Real Questions

Published by
Lion Publishing
Icknield Way, Tring, Herts, England
ISBN 0 85648 347 8
Albatross Books
PO Box 320, Sutherland, NSW 2232, Australia
ISBN 0 86760 352 6

First edition 1982
This edition 1983

The photographs in this book are reproduced by permission of the
following photographers and organizations:
Central Office of Information: 61
Church Missionary Society: 90
Douglas Dickens: 75
IBM United Kingdom Ltd: 73
Lion Publishing: David Alexander: 51
                 Jon Willcocks: 23, 31, 42, 47
Christopher Phillips: 55
Rex Features: 10, 19
Royal Greenwich Observatory: 79
Shaftesbury Society: 87
Clifford Shirley: 82
Tony Stone Associates: 39
Swiss National Tourist Office: 71

D.L. TO: 1546-1982

Printed in Spain by Artes Graficas, Toledo

REAL QUESTIONS

David Field
& Peter Toon

A LION BOOK

CONTENTS

PART 1: LIFE QUESTIONS
In this first part of the book, we try to answer twenty key questions about behaviour. But how do we set about the whole difficult business of making moral choices? The first section, *Choosing right from wrong,* aims to answer that general question. We suggest that you read that section right through first. The chapters that follow pinpoint different areas of life where those choices have to be made. They can be tackled in any order you like.

PART 2: FAITH QUESTIONS
In this part, the scene shifts from morality to beliefs. But the change is not a big one. The Bible knows nothing about belief which does not affect behaviour, and its answers to questions about behaviour are always based on what we believe. The two are therefore tightly interlocked.

1 CHOOSING RIGHT FROM WRONG

BY CONSCIENCE?

Everyone has a conscience. It is the name we give to those deep-seated convictions about right and wrong that we all have. We may not be able to explain them, but we know they are there. Sometimes conscience guides us before the event with warning signals. More often it makes its presence felt by pricking and nagging after we have done something wrong.

Where does it come from?

Conscience is something deeply personal. Mine may be acutely sensitive in some areas where yours is completely indifferent—and, of course, *vice versa*. A pacifist's conscience may allow him to have sex outside marriage, while an army chaplain may see nothing wrong in bayonet practice but everything wrong in adultery. Why are we so different?

The psychologists have exposed some of conscience's roots. In early childhood, they tell us, we absorbed a great many dos and don'ts from other people, especially from our parents. It is those strong moral beliefs that we label 'conscience' in adult life. So there is a sense in which my conscience is not the 'real me' at all, but a complicated mixture of other people's voices from the past. I took them on board when I was too young to work things out for myself, and now I think of them as my own.

Here the social scientist steps in, too. Yes, the roots of conscience may be buried deep in early childhood, he says, but its branches stem from the standards our community impresses on our minds in adult life. Often, those standards are embodied in laws. Take the wearing of seat-belts in cars, for instance. So long as there is no law to enforce it, I don't feel really guilty if I drive without one. But once driving without a seat-belt becomes illegal, my conscience begins to prick whenever I break the law.

Can it change?

Conscience can change, as our convictions about life change. I may have been brought up, for example, in a home where alcohol was strictly banned, but come to believe later that there is nothing wrong with drinking in moderation. My conscience will probably stop me enjoying a glass of wine for a time, but after a while its protests will subside as it catches up with my changed ideas.

Not all changes are for the better, of course. In the New Testament Paul writes about 'liars whose consciences are dead'. He means that conscience's warning signals will weaken and die if they are ignored for long enough. Tell a lie for the first time and you go bright red in the face. But the practised liar can look his victims straight in the eye without a twinge. The voice of conscience can easily be gagged.

Can it be trusted?

A mirror tells the truth about the way you are, but can't give you advice about the way you should be. Conscience can do both, of course. But in some ways it is rather like that mirror, reflecting the values we take in from outside ourselves throughout life. It is vital, therefore, to check up on those values before we trust conscience too confidently as our guide.

It is at this point that the psychologist and the social scientist can help us most. If my conscience sometimes speaks with the voices of those who guided me through childhood, and sometimes through the standards of the society in which I live, I will need to ask myself whether those authority-figures are really reliable. If, for instance, I have been brought up by parents with strong racist principles, my conscience may make me feel uncomfortable when I sit next to someone whose colour of skin is different from mine. But I may need to challenge that voice from the past. The New Testament tells how Peter, with his strict Jewish background, felt exactly that way when he first sat down to a meal with Gentiles—and how he had to ignore those particular pricks of conscience because his new-found faith in Jesus Christ had spelled the end of racism.

This is really just one way of saying that everyone's conscience needs educating. Without knowledge, the voice of conscience stays silent. The fact that a chain-smoker, for example, feels no conscience pangs when he lights up his next cigarette may not mean that smoking is right for him. It may simply show how determined he is to stay ignorant about the effects of heavy smoking on the human body. Conscience can only operate when it is fed with facts.

Christians have their own unique information-centre for the education of their consciences. The will of God is their check-point, especially as it is made clearly known in the teaching of the Bible. Therefore the more a Christian packs his mind with biblical information on right and wrong, the more confidently he can trust the demands of his conscience as a clear echo of God's voice. This may mean that some long-standing feelings of guilt can safely be ignored because, as the New Testament puts it, 'God is greater than our conscience.' On other matters we may develop completely new scruples as we learn (in the words of a great preacher) to 'shiver when even the ghost of a sin goes by'.

The education of conscience takes a lifetime. That fact alone should make a Christian especially cautious when he feels it is right to do things that most other people consider wrong. It should also make him very sensitive to the hurt he may cause to those whose scruples are different to his own.

Jesus put his finger on the adjustment that is needed when he taught his disciples about the meaning of love. The guidance of

SOME CLAIMS FOR CONSCIENCE

● **Too small:**
'Conscience is the product of the nursery.'
Bertrand Russell

● **Too great:**
'Conscience is in all circumstances an infallible guide to right actions.'
Rousseau

● **About right:**
'The wise Christian will give due weight to conscience; it is the natural reaction of his whole being as it has been developed under Christian influences ... Yet he will turn more confidently to other more objective and reliable standards, which he can fully and reasonably accept as his own—the word of God and the example of Christ.'
William Lillie

THE BIBLE TELLS US

● **that conscience normally reflects God's Law:**
'Their conduct shows that what the law commands is written in their hearts. Their consciences also show that this is true, since their thoughts sometimes accuse them and sometimes defend them.'
Romans 2:15

● **but it can give distorted signals:**
'Nothing is pure to those who are defiled and unbelieving, for their minds and consciences have been defiled.'
Titus 1:15

● **and must not lull us into a false sense of security:**
'My conscience is clear, but that does not prove that I am really innocent. The Lord is the one who passes judgement on me.'
1 Corinthians 4:4

'If a man eats meat with an uneasy conscience about it, you may be sure he is wrong to do so.'
Romans 14:23

● **but that God's revealed will carries greater authority:**
'If our conscience condemns us, we know that God is greater than our conscience and that he knows everything.'
1 John 3:20

● **and that we should respect others' scruples, even if we do not share them:**
'Live in such a way that you will never make your brother stumble by letting him see you doing something he thinks is wrong.'
Romans 14:13

one person's conscience must always be balanced by concern for others. It is a dangerous thing to imagine that *your* sense of right and wrong has reached a stage of infallibility which others have missed. The motorist whose conscience allows him to ignore the speed limit in a built-up area, for example, is not really striking a blow for personal freedom in making moral choices. He is being dangerously anti-social. Some horrible things are done in the name of conscience when the interests of others are ignored.

So conscience is by no means infallible. But it is normally a reliable guide if the necessary checks and safeguards are heeded. After all, the alternative is to make ourselves moral puppets, allowing other people to pull our strings and dictate all our choices. And though that might make choosing much

easier, it would take away from us the precious sense of moral responsibility which is an important part of being human.

In claiming the freedom to live by our own convictions, we must not, of course, deny that right to others. One of the Marxist's mistakes is a failure to cope with conscientious objectors. 'There should be no isolated individual, either protruding in the shape of a pimple or ground into dust on the roadway,' claims the communist writer Makarenko. But Christians should not point the finger of blame. They too can be guilty of trying to impose their moral judgements on those who do not share their beliefs.

BY RULES?

The easiest way of all to make moral choices is to live by a set of rules. When you have a problem you can run to your rule-book, flip through the pages till you find a bye-law that fits the situation, read off the solution and then take the necessary action with no further thought or worry.

The trouble is that life's problems are so varied. If you want a regulation to fit every possible occasion, you need a whole library not a paperback. And anyway, there is something deep down in most of us that rebels against living a life trussed up with yards and yards of moral red tape. Even if the computer revolution made it possible to lift the telephone and get instant answers to all our moral queries, we would probably hesitate before dialling the number.

Why are we so suspicious of rules and regulations? No doubt it is partly because of the spirit of the age. Right from childhood we are taught to ask the question 'Why?' whenever anyone lays down the law about the things we should or shouldn't do.

But the real reasons go deeper than that. We can pinpoint some of them by looking at the ways Jesus criticized the champion law-keepers of his time, the scribes and the pharisees.

The danger of living by rules

In the first place, Jesus said, living by rules spells *loss of freedom*. He often used the old Jewish regulations for sabbath observance to illustrate this. The sabbath law in the Ten Commandments was simple enough: 'The seventh day is a day of rest ... on that day no one is to work.' But what did 'work' mean? In an effort to make the law's purpose crystal clear, the religious lawyers had sub-divided work under thirty-nine different headings. Some of the legal hair-splitting was unbelievable! A finger cut on the sabbath, for example, could be bound with a plain bandage but not with ointment. You were allowed to treat a throat infection, but not a fracture.

Jesus had no hesitation in cutting through that kind of legalistic sabbath observance. It had turned a simple law designed to protect the working man's freedom into a straitjacket. A good, general law is like a wall round a house. It restricts and restrains so as to allow those inside to move around more freely. But if the walls are too close (and all the doors and gates are locked), the house becomes a cage. And who wants to live all their life in protective custody?

Another criticism Jesus made of living by rules was that it encourages *low moral standards.* It must have stunned his Jewish audience when he told them that their standards of behaviour must be higher than the pharisees'. 'Oh no, not *more* rules!' they must have muttered under their breath. But Jesus' purpose was not to tie the knots of law even tighter. He wanted to turn their thoughts to a higher kind of goodness altogether.

The trouble with law-keeping is that it props up an attitude of 'I'll do my duty and no more'. Some people attend church Sunday by Sunday in exactly that spirit. They go only because it is a duty prescribed in their personal rule-books, not because they are bursting to worship God with like-minded believers. Some husbands treat their wives that way too, buying a bunch of flowers on their wedding anniversary—not to say 'I love you' but because it is the proper thing to do.

Peter once asked Jesus a question framed in a typical law-keeper's way. 'Lord, if my brother keeps on sinning against me, how many times do I have to forgive him? Seven times?' Jesus answered, 'No, not seven times but seventy

times seven.' Was he making the rule stricter? No, he was telling his disciple to stop counting.

The third and most damaging charge Jesus levelled against living by rules was that it *evades moral responsibilities.* In the parable of the Good Samaritan, the religious people who hurried past the bleeding man were keeping strictly to their rule-books by avoiding contamination. They may even have congratulated themselves as they shut their eyes to his need. Mark Twain once described rigid rule-keepers like that as 'good men in the worst sense of the word'. When a set of rules diverts people from the demands of compassion, something drastic needs to be done about it. In Jesus' time, grown-up children were even opting out of their responsibilities to their ageing parents by quoting from their rule-books. His comment was biting: 'In this way the teaching you pass on to others cancels out the word of God.'

The right place for rules

In the face of such devastating criticism, it would be easy to conclude that all lists of 'dos and don'ts' are more trouble than they are worth. Some people think Jesus drew that conclusion himself when he summed up the law of the Old Testament in his two famous love-commands: 'Love God, and love your neighbour as yourself.' But that is to mis-read him completely. What he did was *first* to distinguish sharply between the broad guidelines of the Ten Commandments (which he upheld) and the scribes' intricate network of bye-laws (which he challenged); and *second* to insist that even the most basic moral rules must be kept in a spirit of love. With those two safeguards, rule-keeping becomes a very useful basis indeed for making wise moral decisions. Let us explore a little further.

For one thing, keeping within a basic framework of rules and regulations can *protect freedom*, instead of threatening it. Sport illustrates that point well. A football match would flow less freely, not more so, if all the rules were scrapped before the kick-off

and the teams took the field without a referee. A game is only spoiled by rules when the authorities add more of them than is absolutely necessary, and when a particular referee or umpire interprets the regulations in an over-rigid way.

Similarly, life itself functions far more smoothly within a simple structure of law and order than it would without it. The law against murder and assault, for example, means (when it is strictly enforced) that I can walk the streets more freely than I otherwise could. Even the mugger would be sorry to see that kind of law go, because his own safety would then be at risk as well as his victim's. What he really wants is a special exception made in his case.

Even those moral guidelines which are not enforced by the law of the land have an important part to play in preserving freedom. Unwritten rules for fair business procedures, for instance, have kept the wheels of industry turning for many years—until fairly recently, that is, when they have become more and more widely disregarded. And the result of that breakdown has been chaos in the business world. Now various new 'Codes of Practice' are appearing which aim to restore those basic standards that businessmen used to take for granted when they dealt with one another.

But another thing a set of basic moral principles can do is to *provide guidance*. Some real-life situations throw up highly complex problems. Seeing your way through to right solutions is like trying to follow the road in a car with a misted-up windscreen. Often the issues are fogged by emotional involvement. It can seem perfectly right, for example, to go to bed with somebody else's husband or wife in the heat of passion—and absolutely wrong in the cold light of the next morning. On occasions like that, a straightforward veto like 'You shall not commit adultery' can de-mist your moral vision at the vital time and help avoid unnecessary tragedies.

But where can we find a set of moral principles we can totally rely

RULES ARE GOOD FOR YOU!

'A great service which rules, and only rules, can perform is the creation of a good, free and happy social climate ... Thus, the observance of a rule against theft in all its forms can do more to make life happy and secure than all the apparatus of State welfare. In a community where there is no need to lock, bolt and bar doors and windows every time you leave your home for more than a few minutes; where property that you lose or leave behind is returned to you or kept to be claimed; where buying and selling everything from a house to a loaf of bread is not a matter of constant vigilance and of knowing all the tricks if you are not to be swindled; where savings that you invest or accumulate against old age will not be embezzled or utterly devalued by negligence or lack of principle on the part of individuals, businesses or governments; where communal amenities will not be smashed or looted time after time; such a society lives in an atmosphere of mutual confidence and lack of strain which is of incalculable benefit to all.'
John Austin Baker

'Law is love's eyes, and without law to give it vision, love is blind.'
James Packer

'I cannot spare the law one moment, no more than I can spare Christ; seeing I now want it as much, to keep me to Christ, as ever I wanted it to bring me to him ... Indeed, each is continually sending me to the other, the law to Christ, and Christ to the law.'
John Wesley

JESUS TAUGHT

● **that keeping God's rules is supremely important:**
'Whoever disobeys even the least important of the commandments and teaches others to do the same, will be least in the kingdom of heaven. On the other hand, whoever obeys the law and teaches others to do the same, will be great in the kingdom of heaven.'
Matthew 5:19

● **and that his own words demand the same level of obedience:**
'Anyone who hears these words of mine and obeys them is like a wise man who built his house on rock ... But anyone who hears these words of mine and does not obey them is like a foolish man who built his house on a sand.'
Matthew 7:24, 26

'If you love me, you will obey my commandments.'
John 14:15

on? Or, to put the question in a slightly different way, where can we discover a source of authority we can completely trust? Christians find the answers to those questions in *God* (the trustworthy authority) and in *the Bible's moral teaching* (which reveals his will in a reliable way). But these are only 'answers' of a general, basic kind. The Bible certainly does not aim to provide made-to-measure rules to fit every conceivable moral problem that can possibly arise in an average person's life-time. What it does do is lay down a limited number of basic rules for living which act as sign-posts, pointing towards the specific solutions we need.

To ask for anything more is to fall into the pharisee's trap. But to ignore the guidelines God has provided is (so Christians believe) to surrender your freedom, and to lose all sense of direction in today's moral maze.

A truck driver listens to strike pickets presenting their case. In an increasingly complex society, we are faced with more and more difficult choices. How do we go about making them?

1 CHOOSING RIGHT FROM WRONG

BY LOVE?

Morality is like an iceberg. The part you see is smaller than the part you don't see. Underneath the visible actions we label right or wrong lies a whole world of invisible attitudes, intentions and prejudices. We get through to that hidden dimension of morality only when we stop asking the question '*What?*' and start asking the question '*Why?*' Take, for example, the husband who buys his wife a box of chocolates. That sounds a highly commendable thing to do—until, perhaps, you begin probing beneath the surface and asking awkward questions about his reasons for doing it. Was it really an expression of love? Or was it an olive-branch to ease his conscience after a first-class row—or even just a matter of habit, because the date happens to be Friday the 30th and he *always* gets chocolates for his wife when the month has five Fridays in it?

One of the most striking features of Jesus' approach to moral questions was the great stress he laid on thoughts and feelings. Time and again he insisted that a 'keep your nose clean' approach to behaviour was totally inadequate. He reached behind the faithful husband's respectable front, for instance, to ask embarrassing questions about the thoughts that go through his mind when he passes a good-looking girl in the street. He by-passed the restraint of a man suffering silently under severe provocation to expose the murderous feelings in his heart— even though he has no intention of translating his anger into action.

According to Jesus, our thought-life is so vital because it is the source of our motives. And a motive is by definition 'something that moves' me. If my inner life is

dominated by motives of lust and hate, in the end they will inevitably show through in my behaviour; just as surely as the pressures of molten lava beneath the cap of a volcano will eventually erupt.

Love—top priority
This is the back-cloth against which Jesus preached his gospel of love. Even the best actions are soured and spoiled, he taught, unless they spring from a loving motive. The apostle Paul expanded the same theme in his famous hymn of love, towards the end of his first letter to the Christians at Corinth: 'If I were to sell all my possessions to feed the hungry,' he wrote, 'and, for my convictions, allowed my body to be burned, and yet had no love, I should achieve precisely nothing.'

As far as moral choices are concerned, this focus on love corrects some of the faults of living by rules that we noticed in the last section. For one thing, love always puts people first. If a neighbour's wife runs to your home for shelter after a row with her violent husband, what do you do when he arrives on the scene brandishing a knife and asking if you know where she is? The rule-book demands 'Tell the truth', and points to an ice-cold decision that might well end in tragedy. But love forces you to look for alternatives which will ensure the woman's safety.

Then, too, love goes beyond duty. If you witness a mugging, you are not acting illegally if you hurry past the scene with your eyes shut. But love drives you to help the victim, even if it means risking your own personal safety. A 'mind your own business' approach to morality may keep strictly to the letter of the law, but it can never pass the love test.

What does love mean?
Unfortunately, love is a very slippery word. The media use it to describe a film star's fifth marriage and to advertise a new brand of tights. 'Making love' is just another way of saying 'having sex' to many people, and 'loving behaviour' can mean little more than stoking up a warm, emotional glow inside. So to

leave someone with the moral motto 'Do the loving thing and you'll never go wrong' is not really much help. It is about as much use as putting a destination on a train departure board, without the time it leaves and the platform it leaves from.

Jesus left his disciples in no doubt at all about what he meant by love. In a nutshell, his kind of loving meant putting someone else's interests before your own. It is the sort of love that looks for no return. 'If you love those who love you, what credit is that to you?' he once asked his disciples. 'Love your enemies, and do good, and lend expecting nothing back.'

So unique is this love that the New Testament uses a special word for it (*agape* in Greek, pronounced 'aga-pay'), to distinguish it from everything else that goes under the 'love' label. There is the love of physical attraction, for example. Basically, that is one person's response to someone else whom he or she finds attractive. ('How did you fall in love with your wife?' 'Well, I only had to look at her, didn't I!') *Agape* is bigger than that. It works where there is nothing attractive or lovable in the someone else at all. In other words, it responds to need, not to merit.

Friendship is another popular kind of loving. But that too has its limitations. Even though it may have no physical dimension to it, friendship has to be shared to survive ('It takes two to be friends'). Again, *agape* is distinctive. It loves on even when it gets no love back. And it is different from family affection, too. That sort of love is limited to a small number of very special people ('I'd do anything for my children'). *Agape* has no such narrow group limits. It embraces all, including needy people in faraway places I shall probably never visit.

This is not to say, of course, that Christianity plays down sex, friendship and family life. On the contrary, it values all of them extremely highly. But it does mean that if I think I am satisfying Jesus' demand to 'love my neighbour' simply by feeling attracted to my marriage partner (if I have one), by keeping up with my friends and by being devoted to my family, I am living in a fool's paradise. *Agape* means so much more than all three put together.

THE TWO DIMENSIONS OF LOVE

● **according to John:**
'This is what love is: it is not that we have loved God, but that he loved us and sent his Son to be the means by which our sins are forgiven.'
1 John 4:10

'If someone says he loves God, but hates his brother, he is a liar. For he cannot love God, whom he has not seen, if he does not love his brother, whom he has seen.'
1 John 4:20

● **according to Paul:**
'Your life must be controlled by love, just as Christ loved us and gave his life for us.'
Ephesians 5:2

'Love is patient and kind; it is not jealous or conceited or proud; love is not ill-mannered or selfish or irritable; love does not keep a record of wrongs; love is not happy with evil, but is happy with the truth. Love never gives up; and its faith, hope and patience never fail.'
1 Corinthians 13:4-7

● **according to Jesus:**
'My commandment is this: love one another, just as I love you. The greatest love a person can have for his friends is to give his life for them.'
John 15:12-13

'Love your enemies and do good to them; lend and expect nothing back. You will then have a great reward, and you will be sons of the Most High God. For he is good to the ungrateful and the wicked.'
Luke 6:35

Love and obedience

But even that only represents half of what Jesus meant by acting from a loving motive. 'Love your neighbour' is just one of the *two* legs on which his love-teaching stands. The other, 'Love the Lord your God', makes the Christian kind of loving even more distinctive.

Jesus spelled out its practical implications by pointing to his own perfect love-relationship with God the Father. 'I have obeyed my Father's *commands*,' he said, 'and remain in his *love*.' In the same breath he told his disciples, 'If you obey *my* commands, you remain in *my* love.' And John, who recorded those words of Jesus, obviously got the message himself, because he wrote in his first letter (later in the New Testament), 'Our love for God means that we obey his commands. And his commands are no burden.' Doing what a loved one wants is never oppressive.

So Jesus deliberately slotted together the two approaches to decision-making we have been looking at in these last two chapters. Many people today assume that living by rules and living by love are alternatives. You have to choose either the one way or the other. But Jesus refused to set them on a collision course. He certainly subscribed to the view that 'love is the greatest', but that did not make him want to throw God's rule-book out of the window. He told his disciples to hang on firmly to both—the rules to give their love direction and stability, and love to keep their rule-keeping sensitive and warm.

BY RESULTS?

Most people try to keep on the right side of the law, and very few would refuse to help a neighbour in trouble if they were actually asked. But apart from crimes and crises, how do ordinary men and women usually judge between right and wrong in everyday life?

More often than not, they do so by making a guess at the future. If someone reproaches you for something you have done, what he usually means is that in his opinion it is likely to have bad results. If you can show him that your action will cause no one any harm—or, better still, that it will do somebody a little good—then, in the eyes of most onlookers, you will have the perfect answer to the charge.

Rule of thumb

Take, for example, the case of a mother who has just found out her teenage son has been sleeping with his girl-friend. If she corners him and tells him in a shocked voice that he has 'done something immoral', she may well get the answer back, 'Why, where's the harm in it? We've neither of us got VD and we've made sure we don't start a baby, if that's what you mean.' Whether that is what she meant or not, unless she can prove to her son's satisfaction that sex outside marriage is likely to have bad *results*, she is unlikely to convince him.

Then again, think of an assembly-line worker with a sensitive conscience, who is on the point of confessing that he has taken home various bits and pieces from the factory to mend his motor-bike. Imagine his friends' astonishment when he tells them what he is planning to do. 'Are you out of your tiny mind? What d'you want to go and do that for? You'll only get yourself into bother. You could even lose your job, and you'll probably make trouble for us.' In other words, the only way to decide whether honesty is right or wrong is to calculate what the *results* are likely to be. Will it pay?

This rough and ready way of making moral judgements has obvious advantages. It would certainly be hard to defend any action which had bad consequences for everyone involved, especially if those results could have been foreseen. And as a method of coming to snap decisions it is wonderfully flexible. All the fuss about telling 'white lies', for instance, disappears when you judge them simply by their results. A lie is right if it helps, and wrong if it harms. It's as easy as that.

Problems

Well, perhaps not *quite* so easy! There are, in fact, many hazards in this particular route to moral decision-making which make it the least reliable of all the options we have been exploring. Here are just three of the major drawbacks.

First, there are big problems in deciding *how to measure results.* To measure anything, you need a standard which everyone accepts. A beer-drinker, for example, expects to be served in pints or litres. If the barman offers him a mug-full instead, he will naturally be rather suspicious. Whose mug—and how much does it hold?

The trouble with measuring the results of behaviour is that no accepted standard exists. 'Personal pleasure' and 'the greatest happiness of the greatest number' are two of the most popular suggestions to have been made. But even they can point to opposite conclusions. For instance, the Playboy addict believes in the goodness of recreational sex because it provides him with a great deal of personal pleasure. But those who know some of his jilted 'playmates' may want to make very different calculations— based on the amount of unhappiness his lifestyle has caused.

Secondly, *all the moral anchor-points of life disappear.* Take theft.

The vast majority of people would agree that stealing is wrong, but if you make all your moral judgements by calculating results, sweeping statements like that lose their meaning. If someone asks you 'Is it wrong to steal?' you have to reply, 'I don't know. I can't tell you whether any act of theft is right or wrong until I see the results.' And the same goes for mercy-killing, rape and everything else. All the old guide-lines vanish. It is as though someone insisted on taking all the labels off the bottles and boxes in your medicine cupboard and then said, 'Work out the right dosage by the consequences.' That may be exciting (and good business for undertakers), but it has obvious perils for non-experts who would much rather be told what to do in words of one syllable.

Then, third, there is the problem of *forecasting the results accurately*. With a lot of help, we just might find a reasonable way of measuring the moral results of our actions. But how can we be certain what those results are going to be? The immediate consequences may be obvious enough, but the further we get from the present the more difficult it becomes to forecast the remote results of anything we do. Who knows for sure what may happen, ultimately, as a result of this lie or that divorce? It is hard enough to prophesy how far the ripples will spread when you toss one stone into a lake, but the situation gets far more complicated when everyone else is throwing in stones too! The world is littered with the human debris of other people's plans which had unexpected consequences. Where right and wrong are concerned, to put all your trust in results is a very dangerous gamble indeed.

Reliable forecasting

This is why Christian ethics places far more emphasis on obeying basic moral rules (interpreted by love and applied by conscience) than it does on calculating results. And yet an appeal to consequences does still play some part in the Bible's moral teaching.

Quite often Jesus himself

backed his moral demands by forecasting the *personal* consequences of a particular lifestyle. What is the profit in selfish hoarding, he asked his disciples, when you die and face God's judgement? There is loss, not profit, if the hoarder ends up in hell! If the greedy man has failed to see any further than his own retirement, he just hasn't calculated the consequences far enough ahead.

It may surprise casual readers of the four Gospels to find how often Jesus used heaven and hell language. He wanted to jolt people into considering the eternal results of the way they lived in the here-and-now. And the Bible sometimes appeals to long-range *social* consequences, too. One of the most interesting examples comes in the fifth of the Ten Commandments, 'Honour your father and your mother, that you may live long in the land.' 'Once you erode the structures of the family,' the commandment says in effect, 'your society will be half-way down the slippery slope to disaster.'

Some modern social scientists would disagree with that. The end of marriage and family life, they would claim, can result in nothing but good. Here, then, is a major clash in the forecasting of consequences. And here, too, is the biggest contribution Christians can make to the 'living-by-results' debate. God, the Christian believes, is the best long-range forecaster in the business. He sees beyond all our personal horizons. And he knows what is on the other side of the social reformer's dreams. This surely means the very least men and women can do, if they are absolutely determined to measure their behaviour by its results, is to take note of the long-range consequences God predicts.

CONSIDERING CONSEQUENCES CAN SWAY MORAL JUDGEMENTS— RIGHTLY OR WRONGLY

'It is not worth stealing from this box because it is emptied regularly.'
Notice on a church collection box

'Prosecutions have been brought against people leaving trolleys in the road or on pathways. Avoid this risk.'
Notice on a supermarket trolley

'Robin Hood was not really stealing at all . . . he soaked the rich to provide assistance and other amenities for the poor.'
Kenneth Greet

'If some of my clients weren't able to obtain sexual satisfaction from me. I believe it likely that innocent women and girls might well be molested and raped.'
A call-girl

'There is a world of difference, hypocritical as it is, between doing something and not being found out and doing something and being found out.'
A politician

'By providing the therapeutic sexual services necessary in our society, they (prostitutes) would leave the streets free and remove the attendant vice, health and crime problems.'
Kenneth Russell

THE NEW TESTAMENT ENCOURAGES ITS READERS TO CONSIDER THE CONSEQUENCES OF THEIR LIFESTYLE

'Do not deceive yourselves; no one makes a fool of God. A person will reap exactly what he sows.'
Galatians 6:7

'You can be sure that on Judgement Day everyone will have to give account of every useless word he has ever spoken.'
Matthew 12:36

'The Son of Man is about to come in the glory of his Father with his angels, and then he will repay everyone according to his deeds.'
Matthew 16:27

'Whoever believes in the Son has eternal life; whoever disobeys the Son will not have life, but will remain under God's punishment.'
John 3:36

ARE THE SEXES EQUAL?

Una Kroll tells a story at the beginning of her book, *Flesh of My Flesh*, which brings this question to life. She needed a new gas cooker. When she had chosen the model she wanted in the showroom, she asked whether she could pay for it over an extended period. 'Certainly, madam,' replied the assistant, 'but I must ask you to get your husband's signature for the hire-purchase agreement.' 'Why?' she asked. 'I have a good job. I can pay my own debts. Why do you need my husband's signature?' 'It's the rule, madam,' she was told. 'Your husband is the head of the household, so he must sign the agreement.'

That, writes Dr Kroll, is just a minor example of sexism. In her case, the situation was made even more ironical by the fact that her husband was unemployed at the time and could never guarantee the payments. It was simply assumed that she, *because she was a woman*, could not take on such responsibilities.

The Women's Liberation movements (in the plural, because many different organizations with contrasting aims meet under that banner) exist to put an end to all discrimination against women. Great social strides have already been made, of course. Women have the vote. They have access to higher education. Their career prospects are far brighter than they used to be, and many are financially independent. But, say the advocates of equality, there are big battles still to be won before the final victory over sexism can be celebrated.

Body and mind
In particular, feminist cries for freedom focus attention on two main areas of life where male domination is still obvious. First, there are chauvinist attitudes to *the female body*. Germaine Greer is typical of many who appeal to biology at this point. When there is only one chromosome's difference (out of forty-eight) to distinguish male from female, she argues, why should women be treated as sex-objects and men as people? Surely a woman must be given the freedom to do what she wants with her own body, and to find her own identity as a person apart from her relationship to men. Hence the bra-burning protests and the indignant graffiti scrawled across nude advertisements by supporters of Women's Lib. Women are not just decorative objects for men to whistle at. Nor are they living incubators for men's babies—which explains why demands for abortion and the right to choose a lesbian lifestyle are also prominent planks in the feminists' platform.

The second major focus of protest turns the spotlight onto *the female mind*. Why should women still carry the brand-image of being impulsive, irrational, emotional creatures, while men are always considered stable, logical and intelligent? The answer, says Women's Lib, is in social conditioning. Right from childhood, boys are taught to look forward to a career, while the starry-eyed goal for girls is marriage to 'Mr Right' and the starting of a family. Later, they may both go on to higher education, but while *he* gets qualified for a profession, all the social pressures on *her* are to find a husband before all the eligible males get snapped up. And then, as a wife, she suffers the mental rape of being reduced to household drudgery while her partner leads a challenging, fulfilled life in the outside world. All that must change!

Christianity—villain of the piece?
Most feminists see the church as a bastion of male domination. After all, both its leadership structures and its concept of the Godhead are overwhelmingly masculine. God is

'King' and 'Father'. Jesus is 'Master' and 'Son'. Who would dream of praying 'Our Mother who art in heaven...'? No wonder Helen Reddy attracted so much Christian hostility when she accepted her Grammy Award with the words, 'I'd like to thank God because She made everything possible.'

This kind of protest is based on a most distorted caricature of Christian teaching. When the Bible refers to God as 'He', it does so to stress the fact that the Supreme Deity is a Person (rather than a mathematical formula), not to distinguish him as male instead of female. The Creator is beyond all distinctions of human sexuality. Jesus made this quite clear when he told the Samaritan woman, 'God is *spirit*, and those who worship *him* must worship in spirit and in truth.'

It may come as a surprise to discover how often the Bible uses feminine word-pictures to describe God. The Old Testament prophet Isaiah is especially fond of picturing 'him' as a young mother, loving and comforting her children. 'I cry out like a woman in labour,' says the Lord through the prophet. 'I will comfort you as a woman comforts her child.'

There is no support in the Bible for discrimination against women. Indeed, the story of creation rules out sexism explicitly. Both men and women are made in God's image, so in their relationship to him neither can be 'more equal' than the other. And in their relationship to one another, the picturesque description of Eve's creation from Adam's rib makes the point that men are never meant to oppress women, nor vice versa. Peter Lombard saw this centuries before Women's Lib: 'Eve was not taken from the feet of Adam to be his slave, nor from his head to be his lord, but from his side to be his partner.'

This is not to say that Scripture ignores the existence of war between the sexes. But it traces the root of the problem not to God's will, but to men and women's joint rebellion against their Maker's instructions. Straight after their first unilateral declaration of independence, God predicted all the hardship and misery that make up the target of feminist protest today. 'You will still have desire for your husband,' he told Eve, 'but he will dominate you.'

Over in the New Testament, the apostle Paul brackets sexism with racism and class discrimination as three examples of broken human relationships that Christ came to mend. And Jesus himself led the way by personal example at this point. He commended female tenacity as a pattern for prayer. He taught in the temple's Court of Women, implying by doing so that they were at least the equal of men in intelligence and spiritual perception. And he astonished a common-law wife by deliberately starting a conversation with her by a well. These things may not strike us as being very remarkable. In Jesus' day they were revolutionary.

Christianity, then, is not a religion that protects the vested interests of male domination. But at the same time it does not draw all the conclusions that the feminist movement would like. In particular, the Bible stresses the *differences* between men and women as well as their *equality*. This will become more clear as we take a closer look at the roles of the sexes inside and outside marriage.

Sexual roles

When the Creator gave men and women their directions for life, his 'Maker's Instructions' (expressed in Genesis I – see quotation) covered the two areas of living which we tend to distinguish as specially male (creative work) and specially female (the bearing and rearing of children). *But that sexist contrast was not there in God's words.* His creation mandate opened up the whole careers spectrum to women as well as to men (which gives clear guidance to Christians debating job-opportunities and equal pay). And it made the bringing up of children father's responsibility as well as mother's.

So far so good, the feminist lobby might say. But here the Bible takes a step further than Women's Lib. As well as opening up the way for women to pursue careers, and inviting fathers to take their share of family responsibilities, Scripture distinguishes a special role for motherhood and home-making. Germaine Greer sees the nuclear family as men's tool to oppress women. She would prefer to replace it with a commune structure where 'my child need not even know that I was its womb mother'. In feminist demonstrations banners are carried with slogans like 'Put Motherhood in a Test-Tube' and 'Washing Diapers is not Fulfilling'. But the Bible is far more positive about marriage and motherhood than that. Nowhere does it hint that a working woman is missing out on the best (though, culturally, very few women had jobs outside the home in Bible times), but everywhere the role of wife and mother is raised to the very highest level of importance. Staying at home and looking after the children is assumed to be one of the most valuable and fulfilling occupations there is.

Putting this biblical teaching together, there can be no objection on Christian grounds when a couple decide to 'reverse their roles', the woman becoming the wage-earner and the man the house-keeper. But Christians should protest more loudly than the fiercest feminist if that decision is based on the idea that home-making is second-rate, unfulfilling drudgery. The fact that only females can bear babies, and that most mothers have strong maternal instincts, makes women different—but not inferior.

It is Paul's description of the marriage relationship that makes feminists most angry. And yet it is this piece of New Testament teaching that sets out the Bible's 'equal but different' formula most clearly. A wife, says Paul, should submit to her husband as head of their marriage. And the husband, he goes on to say (in words that some feminists miss in their rage), should love his wife self-sacrificially.

There is an obvious balance here. Paul does not justify domineering husbands—the type who tape their wives' orders for the day to the cooker before they go off

THE BIBLE STRIKES A BALANCE BETWEEN THE SEXES

● in their creation:

'Then God said, "And now we will make human beings; they will be like us and resemble us . . ." So God created human beings, making them to be like himself. He created them male and female.'
Genesis 1:26–27

'When God created human beings, he made them like himself. He created them male and female, blessed them, and named them "Mankind".'
Genesis 5:1–2

● in their work as managers of creation:

'He created them male and female, blessed them, and said, "Have many children, so that your descendants will live all over the earth and bring it under their control".'
Genesis 1:27–28

● in their standing as Christians:

'So there is no difference . . . between men and women; you are all one in union with Christ Jesus.'
Galatians 3:28

● in their relationship in marriage:

'A wife is not the master of her own body, but her husband is; in the same way a husband is not the master of his own body, but his wife is.'
1 Corinthians 7:4

● in the 'male' and 'female' roles of God:

'You, Lord, are our father, the one who has always rescued us.'
Isaiah 63:16

'You (Israel) will be like a child that is nursed by its mother, carried in her arms and treated with love. I will comfort you in Jerusalem, as a mother comforts her child.'
Isaiah 66:12–13

to work in the morning, because that kind of chauvinist piggery does not square with self-giving love. And there is a clear ring of equality in his words, too. Both husband and wife are on a level in putting each other before themselves.

Why, then, does this New Testament passage jar on us? The reason is that within the equality of marriage Paul identifies a difference. The husband is head, not the wife. The feminist finds the whole idea of headship unacceptable, because so often it works out as male-dominated oppression. When that happens, the wife has to fight for her rights if she is to avoid becoming her husband's door-mat. But Paul's mind is not on rights and door-mats at all. He is thinking of giving, not getting. And he sees no clash between complete self-giving, complete equality and a difference of role and function between husband and wife.

How can it be demeaning for a wife to look up to her husband as head, when he surrenders all he is and has to her in his love? The words 'superior' and 'inferior' just do not figure in that kind of arrangement. So in biblical terms marriage is not an uneasy, unisex balance of power, but a relationship where partners fill different roles, and where they each find their freedom by gladly surrendering it.

2 EQUALITY

ARE ALL RACES EQUAL?

A few Springs ago Nicholas Swart, a white man, lay dead in a Cape Town hospital. He had accidentally stabbed himself with a bread knife. When the ambulance arrived, the driver (who was also white) had told his wife, 'I'm sorry, this is a non-white ambulance. We have two coloured people in here. We can't take him.' Later, a coloured neighbour had offered to take Mr Swart to hospital in his car. But by the time he got there it was too late.

That small tragedy highlights several aspects of the race problem as we see it today in London and New York as well as in Cape Town—the evils of discrimination, the folly of judging between people by their skin colour, the clumsiness of the law and the emergence of Good Samaritans who are ready to break down cultural barriers to meet human need. The fact that in this case 'the biter got bit' shows how complex the whole problem is. In this chapter we will first analyse the issue, trying to get right to the heart of it, and then look at the places where Christian teaching has something to say.

The problem

Race, colour and culture The word 'race' is itself an umbrella term which covers many different distinctions. Sometimes we use it to identify people who share a common birth-place and language (the 'British race' as distinct from 'Italian people'). Far more often, when we talk about *race* we really mean *colour*. A man with a black skin born and bred in Bradford, England, may suffer far more discrimination when he goes after a house or a job than a white immigrant from Germany who doesn't speak a word of English.

Then again 'racial' differences may simply reflect distinctions of *culture*. Arabs fight Israelis in the Middle East and Pakistanis clash with Indians in London, not because the colour of their skins is different, but because they are consciously defending religious and cultural values against real or imaginary threats. Perhaps this takes us nearer to the heart of the problem than anything else. There is something very deep in human nature which suspects strangers. Differences of skin colour, language or culture simply help us to identify the objects of our suspicion.

Discrimination and prejudice The British Race Relations Act defines discrimination as treating one person less favourably than another on grounds of colour, race, or ethnic or national origin. Despite several attempts to tighten the law, independent surveys show how easy it is for determined people to find loopholes in it. If the colour of your skin is not right, you are still likely to find that an advertised apartment or job has mysteriously disapppeared from the market when you arrive to enquire about it. You may also have to pay a higher insurance premium for your car and run a greater risk of being held on suspicion by the police.

It is important, however, to make a clear distinction between discrimination of that kind and racial prejudice. Discrimination deals in actions and words. Prejudice goes much deeper into the hazy world of biased feelings and attitudes. The two are, of course, closely linked (as branch is to root), but they are not at all the same thing. A white hotelier in South Africa, for example, may discriminate against coloured people just to keep on the right side of the law, even though he personally nurses no prejudice against them. A Londoner in the same line of business may be forced to take in coloured people against his will, while his racial prejudice still smoulders beneath a façade of non-discrimination.

This helps to explain why the law will always be weak and clumsy in dealing with race relations. It is possible (though difficult) to legislate against discrimination, because words and actions can be checked and challenged. But prejudice, because it is an affair of the mind and heart, is completely outside the law's range. When you come to think about it, a *law* which tries to enforce right *relationships* is a nonsense. The best it can do is lop off the branches while leaving the roots of the tree intact.

Segregation and integration It is easy to say we are in favour of racial integration and against segregation, but harder to explain exactly what we mean by either. Segregation, for example, comes in two varieties. There is the compulsory sort, typified by apartheid in South Africa, and the kind of voluntary separation that is deliberately chosen by package tour holiday-makers who want to see the sights without exposing themselves to strange food and a foreign language. It may be wrong to *force* people of different races, colours and cultures to stay apart against their will, but does that make it

SOME MODELS FOR RACE RELATIONSHIPS

1. COMPLETE ASSIMILATION
Known as 'the melting pot theory'. All cultural distinctions are deliberately blurred.

2. SEPARATE BUT EQUAL
The theory behind apartheid—'live and let live'. In practice, some are more equal than others.

3. MULTI-CULTURAL
Each group is integrated with the rest, while keeping its own cultural integrity.

4. BLACK MAJORITY/WHITE POWER (OR VICE VERSA)
The minority group makes up for lack of numbers by keeping a firm grip on political and military power.

5. EXCLUSIVE
The attempt to achieve 'racial purity' by excluding (and, if necessary, repatriating) those whose faces don't fit.

right to *stop* them living in ghettos if they choose?

Integration is also an idea with several different shades of meaning. Is it our aim to integrate racial groups as sugar is stirred into coffee, or as bricks are built into a wall? If the former is our goal, we can't rest content until Sikhs cut their hair and wear crash helmets on their motor-bikes. If the latter, we will prefer the 'multi-culture' model which Roy Jenkins has defined as 'not a flattening process of assimilation but equal opportunity accompanied by cultural diversity in an atmosphere of mutual tolerance'. Whichever way we jump, we must be prepared to put some clear content into our slogans.

The Bible and race

Having analysed the problem, we can now try to see it in a Christian perspective. There are three biblical principles which are particularly relevant.

The creation of man The Bible teaches clearly and firmly that *all* people are created in God's image. Here is a basic unity which overrides all differences of colour and culture. It rules out every idea of a racial league-table in which some consider themselves superior to others. When men face their Creator, there are no grounds for racial discrimination. He is absolutely impartial, and Christians are called to be God-like in their attitudes to others.

In the light of our colour-bar mentality, it is especially significant to find that the Bible makes no distinctions between people with different colours of skin. In Bible times it was the black-skinned Ethiopians whose colour stood out as distinctive. The Old Testament notes the difference, but makes nothing of it. And in the New Testament Luke tells of Philip the Jew's meeting with the Queen of Ethiopia's treasurer without any trace of racial embarrassment. Black and olive-skinned, they shared the same chariot and the same Bible with no hint of awkwardness.

GOD'S IDEAL—IN CREATION

'From one man he (God) created all races of mankind and made them live throughout the whole earth.'
Acts 17:26

GOD'S LAW—NO DISCRIMINATION

'For all time to come, the same rules are binding on you and on the foreigners who live among you. You and they are alike in the Lord's sight.'
Numbers 15:15

'Peter began to speak: "I now realize that it is true that God treats everyone on the same basis. Whoever worships him and does what is right is acceptable to him, no matter what race he belongs to".'
Acts 10:34-35

GOD'S RECONCILIATION— ON THE CROSS

'For Christ himself has brought us peace by making Jews and non-Jews one people. With his own body he broke down the wall that separated them and kept them enemies . . . in order to create out of the two races one new people in union with himself, in this way making peace. By his death on the cross Christ destroyed their enmity; by means of the cross he united both races into one body and brought them back to God.'
Ephesians 2:14-16

GOD'S IDEAL—IN HEAVEN

'After this I looked, and there was an enormous crowd—no one could count all the people! They were from every race, tribe, nation and language, and they stood in front of the throne . . . They called out in a loud voice: "Salvation comes from our God, who sits on the throne, and from the Lamb!".'
Revelation 7:9-10

The fact of sin If God made all people equal, how did racial discrimination and prejudice get in to spoil the happy picture? The Bible's answer is summed up in the one word 'sin'.

Sin's main threat lies in its power to divide. As well as coming between people and God, it spoils every kind of relationship between people. And its trade-mark is self-centredness.

In this context, racial prejudice becomes very easy to understand, if not to change. The British psychologist Stafford Clark put it beautifully when he wrote, 'No one is born prejudiced against others, but everyone is born prejudiced in favour of himself.' It is only a short step from this kind of inbuilt human self-interest, which I share with everybody else, to prejudice in favour of the social group to which I happen to belong. It isn't that I wish any harm to other families, but I'll move heaven and earth to make sure that the interests of mine are advanced and protected. I have no prejudice against people of other races (or colours or cultures), but woe betide them if their presence threatens my job, my standard of living or the value of my property! Discrimination (or a ghetto mentality, which is the other side of the same coin) is really the drive for self-protection or self-advancement dressed up in thin disguise.

It is the fact of sin which persuades Christians that all policies of compulsory segregation are wrong. The irony of apartheid is that the word itself means 'separate and *equal*', while the practice invariably leads to *in*equality and *in*justice. The poisonous ingredient is self-interest, *alias* sin, which will always ensure that the equality this kind of policy achieves is really unequal.

People of varied racial origin watch a West Indian carnival in London. Most of the world's great cities now have multiracial populations. This brings great potential for enriching city life, but sadly has often led to discord and violence. What are the roots of racial prejudice? And can racial discrimination be controlled by law?

Reconciliation Jesus' purpose in living and dying was to deal with sin, and so to reverse its divisive effects. That is the heart of the Christian gospel. He came to reconcile people to God, and to heal broken human relationships. Specifically, says Paul, he has smashed all racial barriers, including the biggest, which in Bible times was the hatred that separated Jews from non-Jews. So in the last book of the Bible John catches a glimpse of heaven and sees there a multi-racial congregation, people 'from every race, tribe, nation and language', worshipping in unity at God's throne.

The New Testament leaves us in no doubt that Christians are meant to anticipate heaven in the here-and-now by expressing racial harmony in their church life (which includes both worshipping and socializing together) and by working for integration in the secular world. This kind of integration does not mean sameness. The apostle Paul says 'there is no difference between Jews and non-Jews' in the same breath that he explains how Christ has abolished divisions between men and women—and he was not preaching unisex! The racial harmony of the Christian gospel comes about when men and women from different cultures sing their own songs in harmony with one another. There is no place for the discord of discrimination.

Before Christ's arrival, God had prepared the way of reconciliation by legislating for social justice in Israel's national life. The Old Testament law lays enormous stress on special care for minority groups who would otherwise (human nature being what it is) suffer discrimination. Among those groups, immigrant foreigners stand out sharply. 'Do not illtreat foreigners who are living in your land,' says the law of Leviticus. 'Treat them as you would a fellow-Israelite, and love them as you love yourselves.'

Here is a biblical stimulus to spur Christians to be right in the forefront of those who fight for fair treatment of racial minorities. Protective legislation is as necessary now as it was then, because human nature has not changed with the passing of the centuries. But the Old Testament law strikes a note which is absent from modern statute books. Alongside the familiar 'do not illtreat', it sets the positive instruction 'love'. In other words, it is addressed to the heart. It reaches beyond the law-maker's proper territory (discrimination) to deal with inward attitudes and bias (prejudice).

The Christian gospel bites deepest at exactly this point. Jesus' greatest claim was not to lay down stricter rules and regulations, but to provide new spiritual power to change human nature from the inside. It is this potential that equips Christians to make their unique contribution in the campaign for better race relationships. The gospel does not just aim a fatal blow at discrimination. It cuts out prejudice, which is its root.

EQUALITY AT WORK

It is a disease of the industrialized nations: the slow strangling of the economy by labour disputes, strikes, absenteeism and missed delivery dates. The symptoms are there for all to see. But what is the cause?

Opinions vary. Some put the blame on a shift in the balance of power between management and workers. Correct that, they say, and all will be well. Others think the main problems are technical, especially lack of adequate investment in industry and reluctance to use new technology. But there is a growing conviction among industrialists and commentators that the root of the trouble goes far deeper than that. After six months of 'industrial education' in Britain, during which he joined in many discussions in boardrooms and on the shop floor, Prince Charles reckoned that the technical reasons for economic failure 'make no sense unless you look at them in the context of the one overriding factor in industrial life—*the human being*'. 'The most important point,' he went on, 'concerns communication. Communication rather than confrontation in the field of human relationships.'

Relationships

In reducing the problems of industry to such a basic human level, Prince Charles was not being original. He was building a bridge across the centuries: from today's world of industry to the simpler working life of Bible times.

The Bible has plenty to say about relationships between employers and workers. In particular, it pinpoints two common causes of breakdown which have not lost their relevance with the passing of the years.

There is failure to respect the worth of the individual From beginning to end, the Bible lays enormous stress on the value of the individual person. Every man and woman, says Genesis, bears the precious image of God. Jesus once compared himself to a shepherd who does not shrug his shoulders and say, 'Never mind, there are plenty more', when one of his animals goes missing; he keeps on searching till he finds it. And looking back to Jesus' death, the apostle Paul reminds his readers that each one of them can say, 'the Son of God who loved *me* and gave his life for *me*'.

There are many influences in modern industrial life which erode the individual's sense of worth and value. Some systems of production, for example, come very close to treating workers as though they are merely tools and not people at all. It is hard for a man on an assembly line to feel that he is anything more than a cog in a vast machine, and shift-work often exacts a heavy human toll, including the breakdown of many marriages. It is all done, of course, in the name of efficiency and profit.

The same principles are used to justify take-overs of small firms by multi-nationals—but again the results are very often dehumanizing for employees, particularly when there is little or no personal contact between those who produce and sell and those who pull the strings.

The Bible condemns profit-making if it is at the cost of human interests. It insists that people are always more important than money. With care and ingenuity, the depersonalizing trends of modern industrial life can be reversed. Groups of workers can see a car through the whole assembly process: they can 'create' a car, rather than just add one part over and over again on the production line. So long as personal values are pushed into the shadows, bad industrial relations will always be in the limelight.

The Bible lays great stress on justice It is under this heading that most of its teaching on working relationships fits best. In Bible times the employer held all the power. Working people, many of them slaves, were often pitilessly exploited. Biblical calls for justice are therefore mainly one-way traffic.

Prompt and fair payment of wages is a major biblical theme. 'Do not hold back the wages of someone you have hired, not even for one night,' the Old Testament law insists. 'He needs the money and has counted on getting it. If you do not pay him, he will cry out against you to the Lord.' The prophets leave unscrupulous bosses in no doubt about whose side the Lord is on in this kind of conflict. 'Doomed is the man who builds his house by injustice and enlarges it by dishonesty,' thunders Jeremiah; 'who makes his countrymen work for nothing and does not pay their wages.'

Trades Unions

If that sounds like a modern trade union convenor holding forth on the shop-floor, it should not really surprise us. The Trade Union movement began with clear Christian aims. Some of the earliest pioneers, including the Tolpuddle Martyrs in Britain, were active Methodists. Some union branches are still known as chapels. Until fairly recently shop stewards were still affectionately known as 'the parsons of industry'. They worked hard towards righting the two wrongs we have noted. They met the human needs of individual workers by providing a network of welfare benefits. And they fought injustice in the factories by resisting abuses such as child labour, starvation wages, the seventy-two-hour working week and indifference to safety.

Some would argue that with the arrival of the welfare state the unions have outlived their usefulness. But that is too narrow a point of view. If anything, the position of individual workers in the days of joint-stock companies is weaker than it has ever been.

Without the strength of union solidarity, ordinary working people would undoubtedly be exploited just as harshly today as any builder's labourer was in Jeremiah's time.

This is not to pretend that trades unionists never abuse their power. The Bible links its command to employers to treat their labour force justly with an appeal to workers to give a fair return for their wages. Among other things that means not pilfering materials, and working as hard when the foreman has his back turned as when he is breathing down your neck.

And of course the unions are not exempt from society's dehumanizing pressures, either. Treating management like dirt is really no better than treating workers like tools. And if a trades union becomes very big, it can easily happen that its leaders get out of touch with the rank and file. When things get like that, individual members fail to see much difference between the numbers on their union cards and the figures that identify them on the firm's payroll.

Strikes

A trades union's most feared weapon is, of course, the withdrawal of its members' labour. Strike action has sometimes received a bad press from church leaders. At the turn of the century, for example, Charles Ellicott, Bishop of Gloucester, suggested that all union agitators should be ducked in their village horse-ponds. Much nearer our own time, Archbishop Fisher of Canterbury wrote in a national newspaper, 'I think it is an unrighteous thing ever to strike for money, except possibly when you are starving.'

It would be a mistake to take such extreme opinions too seriously. Many strikes are not about money at all, and even those that are may be morally justifiable. Before making hasty judgements about a particular strike, Christians will want to assess both the *motives* of those who called it and the likely *results* it will have for them and for others.

A strike may very well be motivated by a search for justice. If, for example, a firm's management has failed to implement an agreement or is guilty of some unfair practice, there may be sound moral grounds for a withdrawal of labour. In spite of Lord Fisher's strong words, a grossly unfair wage offer may also justify strike action when all other means of negotiation fail. In answer to cries of 'self-interest', it would not be hard to find cases where people have come out on strike to support a colleague's just cause, often to their own disadvantage. Anyway, it can hardly be morally wrong for an employee to withdraw his labour if he thinks he is not getting a fair price for it, when it is morally right for an employer to take his goods off the market when he considers them undervalued.

On the other hand, the motives behind a strike may be selfish and greedy. In the New Testament, John the Baptist told a group of soldiers, 'Don't take money from anyone by force ... Be content with your pay.' These were working men who could easily add to their wage-packets by bullying tactics whenever they wanted. Their equals today, perhaps, are the dockers, the transport workers and the others whose key jobs give them more bargaining muscle than others. They may be tempted at times to use their industrial power selfishly to squeeze more out of their employers than they should. Unscrambling mixed motives is never easy, but it is a Christian duty to distinguish need from greed before making moral judgements.

Then again, the *consequences* of a strike must be measured as carefully as its motivation before deciding the rights and wrongs of a particular case. Here Christians will want to apply Jesus' 'Good Samaritan' standards .

A strike may bring the strikers themselves rewards—but what about others who may get hurt along the way, including consumers and innocent third parties? The Bible teaches that it is wrong to advance your own sectional interests by making others suffer.

WHEN SELF-INTEREST TAKES OVER . . .

'I saw that all labour and all achievement spring from man's envy of his neighbour.'
The Bible—Ecclesiastes 4:4

'Labour is the commodity of men, as capital is of the masters, and both are allowed to obtain the best terms they can.'
Joseph Hume, eighteenth-century parliamentarian

'Management must remember that workers are individual people with their own dignity, and trades unions must recognize that their vast memberships are more than a mere statistic.'
Malcolm Langton, businessman

'To mistreat the workman as "a piece of machinery" is and remains a violation of his human dignity. Even worse, it is a sin going squarely against the sixth commandment, thou shalt not kill.'
A. Kuyper, theologian

'You have not paid any wages to the men who work in your fields. Listen to their complaints! The cries of those who gather in your crops have reached the ears of God, the Lord Almighty.'
The Bible—James 5:4

'Many resent what is regarded as excessive trades union power and bullying tactics, but few of us would wish for a return to days when the top-hatted mine-owner drove his men underground with little concern for their safety.'
John King, teacher and journalist

'As for the democratic process within a union, everyone knows that power can be exercised by a militant minority.'
Hugh Montefiore, Bishop of Birmingham

'The dangers (of the "closed shop") are of a permanent nature because of the power that becomes available to the few who choose to use the democratic procedures of the trades unions to their own ends.'
Tom Chapman, Secretary-General of the ECIM

'The gaffer who pinches a pen, parks on a double yellow line or fiddles his income tax return; the employee who clocks his mate's card, repairs his punctured inner tube in the works' time, or plays his transistor at the bench . . . the lines of Christian morality are becoming more extended, more blurred, more complex and less distinct.'
Ralph Capenerhurst

Sometimes it may be argued that the hurt is justified by long-term results. A teachers' strike, for instance, may ruin one group of children's examination chances but safeguard future classes by ensuring that they get an adequate supply of good teaching staff. Assessing consequences can be even harder than measuring motives. But it is vital to do both if a fair, Christian moral judgement is to be reached.

So what happens if an employee believes that a particular strike is *un*justifiable, when he has weighed up the motives and consequences as carefully as he can? The Christian answer is that he should not join it. It is not that he must follow the dictates of his own conscience with no regard for anyone else's. His

fellow-workers have a claim on his loyalty too (as the pickets at the gate will no doubt remind him). A chain is only as strong as its weakest link, and collective bargaining relies on collective action for its effectiveness.

The strike-breaker has other moral problems to face as well. What, for example, will he do with the benefits he may gain from the strike he has not supported? Those who are likely to gain from a victory are normally under some obligation to fight in the battle. All these things must be weighed up carefully, as well as the personal harassment he and his family may suffer, before he decides to become a conscientious objector. But if he cannot escape the conclusion that the basis of the strike is immoral, he has no alternative but to opt out.

These extreme decisions will only have to be made, of course, when relationships between employer and employees hit rock-bottom. Strike action is (or should be) the unhappy end of a road which has passed through every other possible alternative first.

Christians owe their faith to Jesus Christ's supreme act of reconciliation. The Bible says they have a corresponding duty to be reconcilers themselves. That will take some into the political arena, to press for new structures that will encourage better communication between the two sides of industry. It will involve all in efforts to bring together those who are better at slanging one another than co-operating. And that in turn will mean full Christian participation in bodies such as trades unions, employers' organizations and works committees that exist to bridge the gap between management and workers.

3 LIFE AND DEATH
IS ABORTION WRONG?

No one is in favour of abortion—except, perhaps, for a tiny minority of medical people who make a lot of money out of it. You yourself may have a friend or a relative who has had a pregnancy terminated. If so, you will know from experience how requests for abortion usually signal personal tragedies. There may be a sense of relief when the operation is over, but no one wants to hang the flags out.

Nevertheless, many people would argue that abortion is, sadly, the best escape-route when an unwanted baby has been conceived. If the mother-to-be is a rape victim, or if she simply forgot to take her pill, she should surely not be forced to bear a child against her will.

There are others, of course, who would strongly disagree with that line of argument. The foetus, they insist, is an unborn child—not a disposable 'it' but a 'he' or a 'she'. So isn't abortion really closer to homicide than to contraception?

Discussions about abortion often get very confused. To find your way through the maze of debate it will help to identify the main points and to consider them one by one.

The woman's life and health

In extreme cases, there may be a straight choice between saving a woman's life and allowing her pregnancy to continue. In these situations the argument for abortion is very strong indeed. If the cost of saving an unborn child is the death of its mother (through cancer, perhaps), most people would agree that the price is too high.

Thanks to advances in medicine, however, this kind of life-and-death situation is now very rare. Far more often the doctors have to decide how big a threat the pregnancy poses to the woman's *psychological* health. These risks are often very difficult to calculate. How do you weigh, for example, the acute trauma one woman suffers when she finds herself pregnant after rape, against the emotional upset another may feel when her career prospects are threatened by an inconvenient pregnancy? The statistics suggest that 'health reasons' are easy to find if the doctor concerned sees nothing against abortion on principle.

It has to be added that abortion is not a sure route to any pregnant woman's psychological well-being. The operation is often followed by feelings of guilt and remorse. And these can lead to far more deeply-seated and longer-lasting complications than the pregnancy itself.

Family stability

An unwanted baby can strain family life to breaking point. That can happen even when the pregnant girl is unmarried, but the pressures increase enormously if a marriage is at risk and other children are involved.

Once again, there is a vast range of circumstances to consider. One young mother may be facing the prospect of adding a probably deformed or defective baby to a family of three already living in two rooms on a low income; while another is convinced that her marriage will break up if her first baby's arrival leads to the cancellation of a planned holiday. How do you deal with requests for termination like these? As with health grounds, the answer given will usually depend on whether the decision-maker has other reasons for approving or disapproving of abortion in general.

Society's interests

When there are too many mouths in the world to feed anyway, why should people be made to have children they don't want? Surely abortion, like contraception, is a weapon we should be using to fight the population explosion.

This kind of argument carries more weight in a debating society than in a clinic. It can be countered (at the same level) by asking equally searching questions about social health. Is it really in any society's best interests, for example, to encourage the view that the unwanted are disposable?

Doctors and nurses

Some doctors choose to specialize in abortion, but the majority do not. In the early stages of pregnancy a foetus looks enough like a baby to make its death and disposal extremely unpleasant. In later stages it may struggle for breath and even cry. 'To perform abortions,' writes one senior British consultant, 'one has to be tough. It is difficult to kid yourself that you are not taking life when you are throwing little arms, ribs and legs into a bucket.' One can hardly blame operating theatre staff who have more sympathy for the foetus than for the patient in these heart-breaking cases. After all, it is they who have to clear up the mess.

Abortion laws usually contain a conscience clause for medical staff with scruples. But these are mainly ineffective. The only realistic alternatives open to a doctor who refuses to perform abortions are to get out of gynaecology or to emigrate. And that in itself raises big questions about the state of the health services in any society with a liberal abortion policy. Whatever the answers, the case for abortion on demand is incomplete unless it fully considers the professional men and women on whom the demands are made.

Foetal life

So far you may feel that the case is fairly evenly balanced. But there is one more factor to take into account. I have deliberately kept it until last because it provides the key to unlock the whole abortion debate. It can be put like this: *When does human life begin?* From your answer to this question, your overall views on abortion will be predictable.

If life does not begin until birth, the foetus can have no rights at all. It is merely part of its mother's body. On this view a cry for abortion on demand makes a lot of sense. A pregnant woman has the same moral right to an abortion as she has to have her appendix out.

If, on the other hand, life begins at conception, the foetus' rights are human rights. It is not merely part of its mother (like her appendix) but an unborn child with a life of its own. Anyone who believes that can only listen to arguments for abortion which begin, '*Although it means the taking of a life*, abortion is justified in this case because . . .'

Most Christians, looking to the Bible's teaching on life before birth,

---

LIFE BEFORE BIRTH

● **From the foetus' point of view**
At about 17 days it has developed its own blood cells.

At about 24 days its heart has regular beats or pulsations.

At about 6 weeks its skeleton is complete, reflexes are present and brain wave patterns can be recorded.

At about 8 weeks its stomach, liver, kidneys and brain are all functioning.

At about 12 weeks it inhales and exhales amniotic fluid.

At about 4 months its genital organs are clearly differentiated; it can grasp with its hands, swim, kick and turn somersaults.

● **From the doctor's point of view**
'It (abortion) is a lonely operation. Although dilatation of the cervix, the neck of the womb, is an operation he (the surgeon) performs many times a week, on this occasion it will be different. He takes that first dilator and is tinglingly aware that he is about to seal the fate of a foetus, to alter history. In other operations the cervix will dilate up readily, but in this operation it will fight, grip the end of the dilator and force it back into his hand. And then at last he will win, and as he does so he will wonder who has lost.'
Rex Gardner, gynaecologist

● **From God's point of view**
'"Before I formed you in the womb I knew you".'
Jeremiah 1:5

'As you do not know how the spirit comes to the bones in the womb of a woman with child, so you do not know the work of God who makes everything.'
Ecclesiastes 11:5

'Thou didst form my inward parts, thou didst knit me together in my mother's womb . . . Thou knowest me right well; my frame was not hidden from thee, when I was being made in secret . . . Thy eyes beheld my unformed substance; in thy book were written, every one of them, the days that were formed for me, when as yet there was none of them.'
Psalm 139:13-16

● **From society's point of view**
'Recently the Soviet authorities have mounted a campaign to stop women terminating their first pregnancies in view of the serious damage this has been found to cause to their health and the chances of their ever being able to complete any subsequent pregnancy.'
The Times (London), May, 1981

favour the second of these views. Nowhere does the Bible say 'You shall not terminate a pregnancy', but it does speak about the unborn child as a person to whom God relates. Sometimes its language is poetic and we must apply it with caution (see, for example, the words from Psalm 139 in the quotation), but the underlying message is clear: *human life begins in the womb*. Terminating a pregnancy means ending the life of a human being. Once that is grasped and accepted, any abortion becomes very hard to justify.

Alternatives to abortion

A strong bias against abortion does not, of course, solve all the human problems raised by an unwanted pregnancy. To say a cold 'No' to a woman in desperate trouble is unloving, and therefore most unChristlike. If she is refused a termination, some other way must be found to meet the personal, family or social needs that prompted her request.

Unfortunately, these alternative means are sometimes very hard to find. Where they are totally absent, some Christian doctors find themselves counselling abortion with a heavy heart—not because a difficult situation somehow makes a wrong into a right, but because all other 'solutions' lead to something worse. Those who disagree with their judgement bear a heavy weight of responsibility. It is up to them to provide the personal and practical support that will make these 'lesser evil' choices unnecessary.

3 LIFE AND DEATH

WHAT ABOUT EUTHANASIA?

Medicine is wonderful—we wouldn't be without it! But in spite of all the miracle drugs and new surgical techniques, people still die. Though most of us don't dwell on the fact morbidly, we know that death will catch up with us one day. And when that time comes, we naturally hope our passing will be as easy and painless as possible.

In that sense everyone is in favour of euthanasia, because the word 'euthanasia' simply means 'dying well'. Over the years, however, the dictionary definition has taken a new twist, until today euthanasia has become a technical term for 'mercy killing' or 'assisted suicide'. We have got used to the idea in animal medicine. When the cat gets a fatal disease, we ask the vet to put it out of its misery, because that seems the most compassionate thing to do. So if the needle is the right way out for an old loved pet, why not for grandma as well? When it is clear that a person's life is nearing its end anyway, isn't it the most loving (and therefore the most Christian) solution to accelerate death painlessly?

To find our way through to an answer it will help to distinguish two different kinds of euthanasia.

Without the patient's consent

When an old lady has been knocked down by a car, or a young motorcyclist gets seriously injured in a collision, it is usual hospital practice to hook them up to all the life-support systems they need for survival until the extent of their injuries can be fully explored. It sometimes happens that brain death is then diagnosed. The patient can

never regain consciousness, but the hospital's sophisticated machinery will keep his (or her) heart and lungs going indefinitely. In that kind of situation (once the diagnosis is beyond doubt), most doctors would switch off the supporting equipment with a clear conscience. They would do so in the belief that they were not killing the patient, but simply recognizing that he or she had already died. Though television and newspaper reports may suggest otherwise, 'pulling the plugs' is not really euthanasia at all in cases like these.

More complicated situations arise when a patient is fatally ill and develops a curable condition. That can happen at either end of life. A baby may be born with acute spina bifida and the paediatric unit has to decide whether or not to operate to close the lesion. An old man with advanced lung cancer may contract pneumonia, putting the doctor in the difficult position of deciding whether or not to prescribe an antibiotic. Relatives may be able to help with the decision-making, but the patient almost certainly cannot do so. Again, most doctors would claim that they are not administering euthanasia if they withhold treatment in this sort of case. Their paramount duty is to promote the patient's overall well-being, and if the process of dying is irreversibly under way any attempt to delay it may be in his or her worst interests. In the poet's words,

Thou shalt not kill, but shouldst not strive
Officiously to keep alive.

All this, of course, is a far cry from the compulsory kind of euthanasia practised by the Nazis in World War II, when they sent Jews to the gas chambers. To 'put down' individuals against their will in the name of eugenics (or any other social theory) is blatantly immoral by Christian standards. The reason will become obvious as we turn to the second, and more widely canvassed, kind of euthanasia.

With the patient's consent

Most of the controversy surrounding mercy-killing concerns voluntary, not compulsory euthanasia. Vigorous pressure-groups are campaigning in many countries for changes in the law of the land which would allow people to sign away their lives in the event of terminal illness or some terrible accident. The main arguments, for and against, can be grouped under two headings:

The demands of compassion When a man longs for death as a welcome release from a painful, useless existence, it may seem harsh and unloving to make him stay alive. Sometimes the highest motives may prompt that longing for a speedy end to life. The philosopher David Hume once wrote: 'Suppose that it is no longer in my power to promote the interests of society; suppose that I am a burden to it; suppose that my life hinders some person from being much more useful to society. In such cases, my resignation of life must not only be innocent but laudable.'

You don't have to be a brilliant philosopher to feel like that! Euthanasia's apparent benefits spread like the ripples from a stone thrown into a pool. The patient is relieved from his suffering. His loved ones are relieved from the mental agony of watching death slowly approach when they can do nothing to stop it. The family are relieved from the strain of long, intensive care (with the hushed children and the sleepless nights). And society as a whole is relieved from the financial burden of supporting one of its members whose social usefulness has passed. Wherever you look, euthanasia seems to be the most compassionate answer to the problem of terminal illness.

Christians naturally respond warmly to any argument from compassion. After all, Jesus himself was often 'moved with compassion' when he met people in need, and he taught his disciples to follow his example.

But Jesus was a realist too. He knew that some apparently compassionate actions mask selfish motives (like the Pharisees' giving to charity, which disguised their desire for self-advertisement). He also distinguished sharply between

WHAT JESUS DID AND TAUGHT ABOUT . . .

● **the value of human life:**
'Aren't five sparrows sold for two pennies? Yet not one sparrow is forgotten by God. Even the hairs of your head have all been counted. So do not be afraid; you are worth much more than many sparrows!'
Luke 12:6

● **the value of an individual human life:**
'What do you think a man does who has a hundred sheep and one of them gets lost? He will leave the other ninety-nine grazing on the hillside and go and look for the lost sheep. When he finds it, I tell you, he feels far happier over this one sheep than over the ninety-nine that did not get lost. In just the same way your Father in heaven does not want any of these little ones to be lost.'
Matthew 18:12-14

'This life that I live now, I live by faith in the Son of God, who loved me and gave his life for me.'
Galatians 2:20

● **the relative values of physical and spiritual life:**
'Whoever wants to save his life will lose it, but whoever loses his life for me and for the gospel will save it. What good is it for a man to gain the whole world, yet forfeit his soul? Or what can a man give in exchange for his soul?'
Mark 8:35-37

'I am the resurrection and the life. Whoever believes in me will live, even though he dies; and whoever lives and believes in me will never die.'
John 11:25-26

THE CARING ALTERNATIVE TO EUTHANASIA

'If dying people experience much physical distress, have no companionship, feel no understanding or are uncertain of adequate care, there will be quite a few who will ask for voluntary euthanasia.'
John Hinton, Professor of Psychiatry at the Middlesex Hospital Medical School

'A very small number of patients have wanted to discuss euthanasia with us. No one has come back to make a considered request for us to carry it out. Once pain and the feeling of isolation had been relieved they never asked again . . . Anything which says to the very ill or the very old that there is no longer anything that matters in their life would be a deep impoverishment to the whole of society.'
Cecily Saunders, Medical Director of St Christopher's Hospice, London

the superficially compassionate offer of an easy way out and the more deeply compassionate solution of a human problem, which often began with a challenge. When he met the rich young ruler, for example—the man who wanted to be his disciple *and* hang on selfishly to his own wealth—it would have been the easiest thing in the world for Jesus to say, 'Put your possessions in store and follow me'. But that would not have gone to the root of the young man's need. It was a deeper compassion that made Jesus demand, 'Sell all that you have',

even though the immediate result was that the man turned away in disappointment.

It is at this level that some of the 'compassionate' arguments for euthanasia wear a little thin. Character, for example, is the fruit of stress, and on that score no sufferer need feel his life is useless either to himself or to those around him. As one doctor put it, 'Those who tend the suffering and dying come to realize what a vital contribution the dying make to the living.' As far as society is concerned, too, terminal care provides the healthy with an opportunity to express unselfish love for the sick. The financial sacrifice involved may be unsatisfactory from a strictly economic point of view, but the compassion it stimulates meets the human need more radically than euthanasia's easy way out. In the Bible, the Old Testament prophets insist that a society's health must be judged by the way it treats its weakest members.

Euthanasia also allows a multitude of mixed motives to find shelter under the respectable umbrella of compassion. Homes for the elderly, for instance, are society's compassionate answer to loneliness and weakness in old age, but 'putting Granny into a home' may reflect selfishness on her family's part rather than love. It would only be a short step from this to 'let Granny be put to sleep' (compassionately of course), if euthanasia were ever to be legalized.

The value of life Those who favour euthanasia argue that life's value lies in its quality. When (through illness or disability) a person's quality of life plunges below zero, he or she should be allowed to accept death with dignity. Death control, the argument goes, is only the other side of the coin to birth control. We don't look on family planning as playing God, so why should we think it is against his will to plan death? We use medicine to interfere with nature when a curable disease threatens life, so why should we insist on nature taking its course when an incurable disease strikes?

Sometimes the Ten Commandments are quoted ('Thou shalt not kill') as the Bible's answer to this point of view, but the word the Commandment uses for 'kill' really means 'murder'. It means the taking of a life unjustly out of hatred or greed—and that doesn't really fit the mercy-killing pattern.

The real problem with this argument for euthanasia, from the Christian angle, is that it measures the value of a human life by a sub-human standard. If people are only sophisticated animals, euthanasia is a logical way out when a person's physical and mental powers have deteriorated to vanishing point. But the Bible speaks about another dimension to human life which it describes as 'being made in God's image'. Among other things, that means every man and woman has the potential to relate to God in a way no other creature can. It implies that we can never write off a living human being as a 'cabbage' simply because he or she is in a deep coma with no prospects of recovery. And it means that euthanasia for people must be put in a completely different category from getting the vet to give our pet an injection.

Euthanasia is not the Christian solution to fatal illness. But, as with the abortion debate, the human problems don't just disappear with the settling of an argument. If mercy-killing is wrong, some better alternative must be found. The hospice movement for terminal care provides such an alternative. Patients are treated as people of value. In all but a tiny minority of cases, their pain is completely controlled by a carefully-balanced, individually-tailored drug regime. Psychologically and spiritually, they are prepared for death as the gateway to new life. They are taught that death will terminate their illness, but not them. The demands of compassion are met at a deep level and the value of a life created in God's image is upheld. It is this kind of intensive caring which quietens the demands for euthanasia —by showing how unnecessary it is.

3 LIFE AND DEATH

DO ANIMALS HAVE RIGHTS?

People differ a great deal in their attitudes to animal life. At one end of the scale stand those who regard everything in the world as raw material for human consumption and treat animals accordingly. At the other extreme, determined campaigners for animals' rights demand that we treat them as sensitively as we treat ourselves. Some of us are not very consistent—happily eating battery-reared chickens, perhaps, while we treat a pet dog or cat as one of the family. We shall see more clearly where the Bible's teaching fits into the picture when we have taken a closer look at those two ends of the spectrum.

Conflicting views

Animal life is raw material for human consumption Whether we would want to put our names to that statement or not, most of us silently accept it in the way we live. Often it is a case of 'ignorance is bliss'. If eggs are cheaper at the shop down the road than they are at the one round the corner, we thankfully pay less, without asking questions about the way hens are treated to make those lower prices possible. Paté and veal make a nice change—if, that is, you can afford them and don't enquire too closely into the treatment of the animals who produced the contents of those plastic containers and wrappers. And it is much the same with the things we wear and have in the home. Sealskin furs, lambskin rugs and ivory ornaments could all tell interesting stories if only we wanted to know.

The truth is that many of us would become vegetarians overnight if we were forced to take a guided tour round a well-run abattoir. If the trip was extended to take in a battery broiler-house, a calf-rearing factory, an experimental station for developing new cosmetics and a circus training session, some life-styles might change very rapidly indeed!

Is it just misguided sentiment that makes most people want to stay ignorant about these things? The answer must be 'yes', if animals are really no more than raw material. No one objects on moral grounds to the methods a farmer uses to produce a larger and better grain crop, providing there is no risk to the consumer. If a chicken or a calf is merely a commodity, a 'natural asset' for human consumption, it is illogical to object to the way they are reared, providing the end-result is safe, better-quality meat. And if you think this line of reasoning is far-fetched, it is possible to find Christian opinion to back it up. The so-called 'Black Stocking Calvinists' of Holland, for example, taught that the way people treat animals is a matter of complete indifference, because only people have souls.

Animal life is of the same value as human life   Conservation pressure groups have mushroomed in Western society during the last decade or two. Many of them are frankly man-centred, warning us that if we do not make less careless use of our resources we shall have nothing left to consume in the foreseeable future. That is really only a more refined statement of the point of view we have just been examining. It puts animal life on the same level as library books. Those who consume the resources (like those who borrow the books) must think of others who come next in the queue.

Some, however, want to take us much further than that. Mankind, they argue, is part of nature. He shares a common 'life force' with the rest of the animal world. It is blatant human arrogance to distinguish 'higher' from 'lower' forms of life. The value of a hippopotamus is the same as that of a man, because all life is sacred. And for that reason it is always

wrong to take animal life—whether it is to feed ourselves, to clothe ourselves or to protect our health.

This point of view finds a vigorous expression in some Eastern religions, and it is no accident that a fresh interest in those religions has coincided with a growing concern for animal rights. Several leading Christian spokesmen have been powerfully attracted by their message. Albert Schweitzer, for instance, developed his 'reverence for life' teaching so radically that in the end he was even reluctant to swat flies in his operating theatre. And Hugh Montefiore, an influential Anglican bishop, writes: 'the history of Christians' exploitation of nature makes a sorry story compared with Jain and Buddhist attitudes towards our fellow-creatures on this earth.'

The Bible's teaching

The Bible steers us, clearly and positively, between the two extremes we have been considering. It teaches us that animals have more value than things, but less value than human beings.

The value of animal life   The way Jesus used farming methods to illustrate his teaching helps us to see animal life in its right perspective. The good shepherd, he taught, has a personal relationship with his flock. He gives his sheep names and knows each one of them individually. Unlike the man who is only in the job for the money, he cares for his animals enough to risk his own life when theirs is threatened. He notices when just one out of a hundred goes missing and he sacrifices his time and comfort to find it.

The attitude to non-human life which this Gospel teaching highlights is reflected in the rest of the Bible. God, as Jesus described him, puts a higher value on birds than men do. In New Testament times, one penny would buy two sparrows, but for two pence you could get five. The 'bonus bird' might not mean much to the salesman, but God never forgets it.

Right through the Bible

mankind's destiny is bound up with the rest of creation. After the Flood, God's promise of life to Noah took in 'every living creature' as well. The Old Testament law strikes the same note by including specific regulations for animal welfare alongside rules for safeguarding human rights. And when the apostle Paul describes the world's last days when 'God will glorify his children', he makes it quite clear that animals will not be left out of the picture. 'Even the things of nature like animals and plants,' he wrote, 'groan in sickness and death as they await this great event.'

Against this biblical background, it is obviously sub-Christian to regard animal life as just so much raw material. Progress in technology has revolutionized farming methods since Bible times, but God's caring concern for his creation needs to find as clear an expression now as it did then. It may be difficult to reconcile the world's need for more food with a proper respect for the animals who provide so much of it, but Christians must insist that the effort is made. To focus so narrowly on human welfare that the dignity of animals is ignored insults the God who made them both.

Human life and animal life Although the Bible sets a very high value on animal life, it does not jump to the conclusion that human rights and animal rights are identical. Jesus himself made a clear distinction between the two when he taught about the God-like care we should take of animals and birds. The good shepherd, he said, will risk his life for his flock, but 'a man is worth much more than a sheep'. And though God does not overlook a single sparrow, human beings 'are worth much more than many sparrows'.

This distinction goes right back to the creation teaching of Genesis. God's very first command to mankind put us in charge of the rest of creation, ordering us to bring it all under human control. That does not give people the right to treat animals like dirt, but it does mean, among other things, that they may be killed for human food and for human safety. The Bible is quite specific about both. If we human beings insist on leaving nature strictly as we find it, we are abdicating our managerial responsibilities. And the result (as we can see from some parts of the world where it has been tried) is not that animals are drawn up to our level. Without proper management both we and they are dragged down into chaos.

In the light of this biblical teaching, no Christian need become a vegetarian as a matter of principle. 'Everything that lives and moves will be food for you,' God told Noah, after the Flood. 'Just as I gave you the green plants, I now give you everything.' Nevertheless, a proper respect for animal life will reach right into the kitchen. The law of Moses drew this fine distinction sharply when it commanded, 'Do not cook a goat in its mother's milk.' There was nothing wrong in eating goat meat, but everything wrong in boiling a young animal in its own mother's milk. A modern parallel, perhaps, might be fattening pigs on bacon rinds.

Though the Bible says nothing about vivisection, the same general principle can be applied to cases where animals are used for laboratory experiments. No animal should be used in any experiment if an alternative method exists, or if the purpose of the experiment is not closely and necessarily linked with vital medical research. But where there are no alternatives (assuming that such is ever the case), even vivisection is morally justifiable in order to alleviate human suffering.

Christians need, then, to keep two basic principles in mind when they face issues which demand a value-judgement on animal life. According to the Bible, humanity's God-given managerial role allows us to eat animal flesh, harness animal labour and take animal lives in the interests of human health. But respect for animals as fellow created beings should stop us treating them callously. In practice that means striking a balance between efficient food production

ABUSING ANIMAL LIFE

● **for food:**
'There is a real danger that large-scale intensive methods involving great numbers of animals, possibly in surroundings which are uncomfortable to man, can lead to a debasement in the stockman's attitude to the lives for which he has a responsibility.'
The Brambell Report. 1965

'The veal producer's ultimate aim is to fulfil the snob demand, made in all innocence by the public, for a white meat. To this end the calf is immobilised by a collar round its neck secured by a very short tether to two bars, enabling it to slide up and down but not permitting it any movement. It is on slats, often in near darkness, sometimes in a crate.'
Ruth Harrison

● **for research:**
'Deliberately to destroy animals, to maim them or to cause them unnecessary pain without a positive gain for mankind which out-weighs that pain, is wrong and even then there must be the proviso that the gain cannot be procured by any other means.'
Herbert Waddams

● **for sport:**
'When will we reach the point that hunting, the pleasure in killing animals for sport, will be regarded as a mental abberation?'
Albert Schweitzer

● **for luxury goods:**
'Philippi's fur seals of Juan Fernandez island off the Chilean coast were three million strong in the late 1700s. Only fifty have survived man's greed for pelts.'
John Klotz

and farming methods which treat animals as commodities. It means allowing living things to be used for research into disease only when the same results cannot be obtained in other ways. And though animals may be killed to conserve crops and health, it surely means that the Christian should be the first to protest when they are baited or hunted in the name of sport.

4 WORK AND LEISURE

WHAT ABOUT LEISURE TIME?

'I did enjoy the concert, my dear,' said the old lady enthusiastically. 'Tell me, what do you do for a living?' The young pianist was lost for words. The truth was that she played the piano for her living. She was a professional. Others (like the old lady) might look on music as a leisure activity, but as far as she was concerned it was her bread and butter.

That incident illustrates very well how difficult it is to pin down 'leisure' by a simple definition. You certainly can't do it by making a list of so-called leisure activities. Whatever you put on such a list—cooking, singing, stamp-collecting, sport, there will always be someone who does that particular thing to earn his or her living.

Other attempts at defining leisure run into similar difficulties. Most people, for example, think of their leisure-time as the time they have left over from their paid jobs. But if work means 'paid employment', being a student or a housewife becomes a pastime. Just try telling them that when exams or spring-cleaning are on the go! Again, for most people leisure means rest and relaxation, but there are those who exert themselves far more in their leisure activities than they do in their jobs. (A paid model might advertise beds by lying on them in shop windows between Monday and Friday, and then go canoeing at week-ends!)

For the purposes of this chapter I am going to assume that leisure covers the things we do, or don't do, outside our main occupation in life (whether we're paid for it or not). But as a definition even that has its loop-holes. What do we make, for example, of the press photographer who takes holiday snaps or the garage mechanic who builds stock cars for fun?

Leisure and vocation

Making water-tight definitions can be just a word-game, rather like doing cross-words or playing scrabble. But in this case, the discovery that 'leisure' is such a slippery idea is much more important—in fact it provides a key to unlock the distinctively Christian approach to the leisure theme. And the name on the key is 'vocation'.

The word 'vocation' is often used very narrowly, as if it applied to some jobs and not others. But an even more common short-sighted understanding of vocation limits its meaning to work. On this view, a surgeon temporarily leaves his calling when he shuts the door of his consulting room, and the typist opts out of her vocation for a couple of days when she puts the cover over her typewriter on a Friday evening. In other words, our leisure time is leave of absence from our vocation.

This is a far cry from the Bible's teaching. If, in Christian terms, vocation means 'God's calling' it covers the whole of life, not just the part we label work. The Oxford Dictionary highlights this difference in outlook very well when it describes leisure as 'time at one's own disposal'. According to the Bible that is a meaningless distinction. 'Thou art my God. All my times are in thy hand,' sang the Psalmist. Christianity assumes that every minute I have, whether I classify it as work or leisure, belongs to God. To put it crudely, his vocation covers my vacation.

Putting up the umbrella of vocation over leisure has two important consequences from the Christian point of view. In the first place, it means that *leisure ought to be planned.*

That deserves an explanation. The idea of planned leisure may bring to mind holiday camps with early morning rising bells, or conducted coach tours where the tourists are at the mercy of their driver! Some people enjoy that sort of thing, but to others it amounts to *anti*leisure—a stifling of freedom which kills all prospects of a carefree, relaxed holiday stone-dead. Why not just get in the car and go?

Treating leisure as part of vocation doesn't necessarily mean planning of that 'others know best' variety. What it does mean (again, from a Christian angle) is that we submit *all* our lives to God's direction, so that our leisure time assumes the same sense of positive purpose as the time we spend at work. To use freedom language, being at leisure doesn't just mean freedom *from* the chores of work (which may lead straight to boredom), but freedom *for* something different but constructive. The answer to the question 'Freedom for what?' will naturally differ from person to person, but wherever it leads it will involve careful planning.

The second consequence of this 'vocational' view of leisure is that *unemployment can be viewed positively.* If you limit your view of vocation to a paid job, it becomes very hard to see anything positive at all in redundancy and early retirement. It is all too easy to think of yourself as washed up and useless the day after you get paid for the last time. But if you look on leisure time (whether enforced or not) as part of your overall vocation, it becomes possible to ask positive questions like 'Where can I make my best contribution to society as an unemployed person?' or (if you have Christian faith) 'What does God want me to do with my life now?' That is not, of course, to whitewash the defects of political structures which allow unemployment to flourish. But it does point towards some positive, realistic alternatives for people who find themselves without a job against their will.

For most people life is no longer 'all work and no play'. We have more time to use elsewhere than in the work of job and home. Hence the mushrooming of leisure activities – sports, hobbies, entertainments; some we just watch, some we take part in ourselves. But is our leisure merely the fag-end of life? Or is it as important to our full humanity as anything else we do?

CONTRASTS

The Oxford English Dictionary:
'*leisure*—the state of having time at one's own disposal.'

The Bible:
'My times are in your hands.'
Psalm 31:15

Algernon Swinburne:
'O pale Galilean, the world has grown grey from thy breath.'

The Bible:
'Jesus said, "I have come in order that you might have life—life in all its fulness".'
John 10:10

Joy Davidman:
'How many thousands picture Christianity as something old, sapless, joyless, mumbling in the chimney corner and casting sour looks at the young people's fun? How many think of religion as the enemy of life and the flesh and the pleasures of the flesh; a foe to all love and delight? How many unconsciously conceive of God as rather like the famous lady who said, "Find out what the baby's doing and make him stop"?'

The Bible:
'Your presence fills me with joy and brings me pleasure for ever.'
Psalm 16:11

Harvey Cox:
'For *Playboy*'s man, others—especially women—are for him. They are his leisure accessories, his playthings.'

The Bible:
'The right thing to do is to keep from eating meat, drinking wine, or doing anything else that will make your brother fall.'
Romans 14:21

Practical guidelines

So far we have been trying to identify a distinctively Christian approach to leisure. If a person really lives in tune with this approach, there are three main practical effects that will result.

Rest Leisure is not the same thing as inactivity, but it should include it. That is a principle written into the heart of the Bible's teaching. We don't really need the Bible to reinforce it—after all, most of us spend about a third of our lives asleep, but both Old and New Testaments make sure that the point doesn't escape us. 'You have **six** days in which to do your work, but the seventh day is a day of rest,' says the fourth commandment. 'Let us go off by ourselves to some place where we will be alone and you can rest for a while,' said Jesus to his disciples.

Some people with a very high sense of vocation have a very low view of rest. The workoholic businessman secretly despises those who think they need annual holidays. The church minister feels proud if he can't remember when he last had a day off. But according to the Bible both of them are wrong. A doze on a sun-lounger is just as much part of their vocation as three hours' overtime.

It is worth a paragraph in passing to note that watch-dog organizations like the Lord's Day Observance Society often do not deserve the negative image they are given. The protests against Sunday activities sometimes appear as attempts to interfere with the freedom of the individual, when in reality they are aimed at powerful organizations that try to erode ordinary people's leisure time.

Enjoyment Again, some who take their work most seriously make very little room in their lives for any kind of entertainment. An afternoon spent at a sports fixture or an evening at the cinema are, to them, so much time wasted. Sometimes a religious veneer is added to give this kind of attitude the impression of super-dedication. The great Methodist pioneer John Wesley, for example, wrote in the rules of the school that he founded, 'There will be no games, for he that plays when a boy will play when a man.'

The Bible, however, has a much higher view of enjoyment than some of its preachers allow. No one could fault the apostle Paul with lack of dedication, but it was he who described God as the one 'who generously gives us everything for our enjoyment'. And though Jesus himself was so dedicated to his mission that he went to the cross in order to fulfil it, one of his most irritating habits, as far as his critics were concerned, was that he kept enjoying himself. He went to the wrong kind of dinner-parties, turned water into wine at a wedding reception and laid himself open to the charge of being 'a glutton and a heavy drinker'.

Enjoyment of ordinary things is built into the overall Christian view of vocation. The Bible warns us not to make pleasure into a god nor to seek selfish satisfaction at others' expense, but these are vetos on unloving behaviour, not on having a good time. There is no biblical encouragement for those who look down their noses in pious disapproval when Christians use their leisure time to enjoy themselves.

Fullness Jesus promised his disciples, 'I have come in order that you might have life—life in all its fullness.' If we ask what he meant by 'fullness', the way he dealt with people gives us the clue. He was concerned, above everything else, for their spiritual well-being (their 'salvation' and 'eternal life', to use New Testament language). But his love did not stop there. He showed a deep concern for the health of their bodies and minds too. In other words, the fullness of life that he promised was a whole-life affair—something that affected body and mind as well as soul.

This concern of Jesus for 'fullness' or 'wholeness' provides helpful Christian pointers for the way we can plan our leisure time positively. If, for example, my job involves very little physical exercise, my leisure time should include it. If I find little scope for initiative or creativity at work, I should look for leisure activities which will fill that gap. If I rarely meet people in the course of my work, I should make time to do so in non-working hours (because making personal relationships is part of being whole). The exact prescription will differ from person to person, but the principle is the important thing. Becoming 'whole people' and growing into 'fullness of life' under God's direction are just further Christian angles on vocation.

So the Bible encourages Christians not to divide their time into compartments labelled 'work' and 'leisure', but to see their lives as all-of-a-piece under the banner headline of vocation. This means that leisure will be carefully planned (like everything else); that it will include opportunities for rest, relaxation and enjoyment; and that it will reflect Christ's overall desire and promise that his disciples should lead whole, full lives under the direction of his Spirit.

4 WORK AND LEISURE

IS ANY JOB BETTER THAN NONE?

Some people genuinely enjoy their work. But many do not. In a boring job it is all too easy to develop tunnel vision as a defence mechanism. You get through the working week by focusing on week-ends, the working year by deciding where to go on holiday next, and your working life by looking forward to the bliss of retirement. If the chance comes to retire early on generous terms, you accept a golden handshake gladly. After all, the drudgery of a job is only the desert which separates the more pleasant oases of life, and the less of it you have to get through the better.

A positive approach

It is at this very basic level that Christian teaching makes its first contribution to an overall view of work. Having a job, the Bible insists, is not a necessary evil but a positive good.

God made us to be workers. That is one of the things that comes out most clearly in the Bible's description of the world's beginning. Men and women together were entrusted with the management of the rest of creation. (The inclusion of women may surprise some who think the fight for working women's rights began in the twentieth century!) And their managerial role did not just mean sitting behind a desk and pulling administrative strings. It involved manual labour too, as Adam no doubt found out when he was put in the Garden of Eden to cultivate and guard it.

Behind this biblical imagery lies the claim which gives the Christian approach to work its positive character. Working is a vital part of what it means to be human. The other side of the coin, of course, is that a man becomes a little less

human if he does not work. This is the reason for the Bible's strong condemnation of laziness. 'Lazy people should learn a lesson from the way ants live', wrote the author of Proverbs (with a twinkle in his eye, no doubt). 'How long is the lazy man going to lie in bed? When is he ever going to get up?' Paul was less humorous and more direct when he found Christians making spiritual excuses to avoid work. His solution was simple—'Whoever refuses to work is not allowed to eat.'

Unemployment is in no way the same as laziness, of course. Most people who cannot find paid work would gladly surrender their place in the dole queue for some kind of satisfactory employment. Christians can never accept rising levels of unemployment without a protest. No amount of redundancy pay can fill the gap left in any human life by the lack or loss of a rewarding job. Paul's hard words were aimed at people who *could* get jobs but preferred to avoid them, not at those who wanted work but could not find it.

Vocation

In today's world it is sometimes hard to find any kind of work, and complaints about a boring job often reflect a person's frustration at not being able to find the sort of work he or she really wants. Naturally it is difficult to find any deep satisfaction in doing something you regard as second-rate. Nevertheless, many people do find themselves with some degree of choice. Most schools include a 'careers' slot in their curriculum, and it is still common to talk about 'finding your vocation in life'.

At this level, too, Christianity has a distinctive contribution to make. The meaning of 'vocation' is 'calling', and the Bible adds to that instinctive feeling most of us have (that there is a small niche somewhere in the world with our name on it), by pointing us beyond the calling to the Caller. In other words, it makes vocation something personal by linking it with God. Faith holds on hard to the conviction that God not only knows and loves us, but also has a detailed plan for our lives. Every piece of life's jig-saw is specially shaped to take its place in the Designer's pattern, and work is one of those pieces.

That vision naturally adds a new dimension of importance and excitement to the tedious business of job-hunting. The skills I tout round potential employers are God's special gifts to me, designed to be used in a way that he planned long before I knew I had them. Even a job that has to be taken on reluctantly as a stop-gap measure will turn out to be part of the practical or psychological equipment needed for the unknown (but God-planned) future.

Measuring value

One of the difficulties about using vocation language today is that it tends to distinguish some jobs from others. If you are something like a doctor, a teacher or a social worker, you can use the up-market jargon of 'pursuing a vocation', but if you work in an office or a factory you just have an 'ordinary job'.

This kind of distinction is foolish, of course, especially if it implies that some jobs are more valuable than others. The man who empties dust-bins conscientiously is making as great a contribution to community health as a highly-qualified surgeon, when you come to think about it, and think what happens when the power workers go on strike. All the same, depending on where you live and work, you may find yourself looking down on manual labour as beneath your dignity, or despising office pen-pushers as people who never get their hands dirty. Some long for 'creative' work, while others sneer at that kind of occupation as socially useless.

The superiority of white-collar jobs to manual labour was a feature of non-Jewish life in Bible times. But the Bible will have none of this. It describes God as a manual worker who shapes his raw material like a potter elbow-deep in his clay. Other religions would have regarded that description of the Supreme Deity as blasphemous.

FOUR THINGS THE BIBLE SAYS ABOUT IDLENESS:

● Depending on others when you needn't

'Our brothers, we command you in the name of our Lord Jesus Christ to keep away from all brothers who are living a lazy life . . . We were not lazy when we were with you. We did not accept anyone's support without paying for it . . . We kept working day and night so as not to be an expense to any of you.'
2 Thessalonians 3:6-8

● Failing to provide for others when you could

'If anyone does not take care of his relatives, especially the members of his own family, he has denied the faith and is worse than an unbeliever.'
1 Timothy 5:8

● Meddling in other people's affairs when you shouldn't

'They also learn to waste their time in going round from house to house; but even worse, they learn to be gossips and busybodies, talking of things they should not.'
1 Timothy 5:13

● Failing to work for social change when you should

'How terrible it will be for you that stretch out on your luxurious couches, feasting on veal and lamb! . . . You drink wine by the bowlful and use the finest perfumes, but you do not mourn over the ruin of Israel.'
Amos 6:4, 6

FOUR THINGS CHRISTIANS HAVE SAID ABOUT UNEMPLOYMENT

'It seems to me that the God I believe in, the Creator God who has given all people gifts to be developed and used, is indignant at a society which simply allows people, in a sense, to rot and says to them, "There's nothing we need you for"'
David Sheppard, Bishop of Liverpool

'To be unemployed can be a great blow to a man; it is not just the loss of earning power, but also the concept of being a man that is attacked. Even though being made redundant is manifestly the result of economic forces beyond the individual worker's control, he experiences it as a personal attack.'
Tony Walter, sociologist

'I tended to waste time rather a lot at first. It's easy to fill a month or two but really difficult when that stretches to a year or two. And you do need to use your time well to avoid extreme boredom.'
Colin Furfie, unemployed physicist

'I believe God is saying to the church: "I want to get in there among the unemployed. They are of value to me, they are precious to me. I've got a job for them to do".'
David Pawson, Baptist minister

Jesus, too, was a working craftsman for all but the last three years of his working life, and in his day carpenters and joiners had no power-tools to ease the physical demands of their job. Swinburne's picture of the 'pale Galilean' just does not fit the labouring Jesus of the New Testament.

The whole Bible, in fact, refutes the idea that some jobs are more worth-while than others. In the New Testament, Paul has some critical words for those who scramble for what they think are the key jobs in the church. Using the human body as an illustration, he

points out that it is often the parts we overlook that perform the most vital functions. And the same is true of the workaday world. It is an important part of Christian teaching that all jobs are on the same level as far as value is concerned. The man on the assembly line has a vocation just as much as the archbishop in his cathedral.

Incentives

What is it that makes people work hard? The most obvious answer is money. There are many other powerful factors, of course—such as a desire for promotion or the satisfaction of doing a job well, but the financial inducements of piece-rates and productivity deals speak a language most ordinary people understand best. Even in Soviet Russia, where the money-motive is deplored, the private land which farmers are allowed for their personal profit is many times more productive than the publicly-owned acres they cultivate.

The Bible does not condemn financial gain (providing it is not made at others' expense) but it offers an even more powerful incentive to Christian workers. In Paul's words, 'Whatever you do, work at it with all your heart, as though you were working for the Lord and not for men.' Here is the specifically Christian stimulus which makes it possible (though never easy!) to tackle the dullest job whole-heartedly. Here, too, is the key to a positive and Christian ambition. Work done for someone you admire will always be done best. And Christians, say the Bible, should constantly be aware that their work, whatever its character, is primarily done for Christ.

Some people suggest that modern working conditions make nonsense of this New Testament teaching. Is it not unreasonable to ask an assembly-line worker to go through the motions of his monotonous job with the high-flown ambition of serving Christ? And are secretarial staff who work in small, noisy, badly-ventilated offices any better placed to respond to that other-worldly inducement?

Treating working people as pieces of machinery is certainly a violation of human dignity, and should be resisted by Christians for that reason alone. Employers have a responsibility to their labour force, as well as to their firm's customers and shareholders. Something has gone badly wrong if work is structured only for profit, and not for the benefit of those who do it. Nevertheless, the New Testament's incentive to work wholeheartedly was not addressed to men and women with fulfilling jobs. It was directed at slaves, and their working conditions were far from congenial.

They had no security against instant redundancy (or worse) and no union power to protect them from unscrupulous employers. The thrust of the Bible's teaching at this point is that Christian working people should be as highly motivated when the conditions are bad as when they are ideal.

Here, then, are the most distinctive features of a Christian attitude to work: the special incentive of serving Christ, plus a personal sense of vocation, stemming from the conviction that work itself is not humanity's supreme indignity but one of the most fulfilling human activities the Creator has designed.

5 MONEY

CAN YOU BE RICH WITH A GOOD CONSCIENCE?

With a title like that, this section will probably be the least-read in the whole book! After all, who can be called 'rich' these days? Most of us are happy if we can just keep pace with inflation, keep up with the instalment payments and keep the 'overdrawn' symbol off our bank statements.

Nevertheless we are remarkably rich when we stop to think about it. 'Wealth' and 'riches' are relative terms, like 'poverty' and 'need'. In other words, the way you describe yourself depends very much on the person you measure yourself against. As a Londoner living in outer suburbia I am poverty-stricken compared with some of my neighbours who have gas-guzzling cars (at least two), swimming pools in the garden and all the latest as-seen-on-television electronic gadgets. But compared to the drought-stricken African children I see on my colour TV, I'm a millionaire. And even if you watch in black and white (or not at all), the fact that you have bought this book means that you have enough money for essentials such as food and clothes—and books!

Possessions—right or wrong?

The sight of starving children doesn't just tug our heart-strings. It makes us feel uncomfortable, and even guilty. It also brings to Christian minds the scathing sarcasm of Jesus when he said 'It is much harder for a rich person to enter the Kingdom of God than for a camel to go through the eye of a needle.' In other places, too, the New Testament seems to suggest that the right Christian attitude to money and possessions is to get rid of them. Jesus told one young man who had more than most, 'Go and sell all you have and give the money to the poor.' He ordered his disciples to travel light, with no money in their pockets. And after his death and resurrection the members of the young church in Jerusalem sat very loose to the things they owned. 'No one said that any of his belongings was his own', comments Luke, 'but they all shared with one another everything they had.'

If we tune in to biblical teaching like this it does sound as though monks and nuns (with their vow of poverty) and missionaries who 'live by faith' are the only Christian people today with enough courage to take Jesus at his word. But turn the tuning knob a little further and we hear the Bible speaking with a different voice. Jesus himself never taught that it was sinful to be rich. He even told a parable in which the characters who made the most money were not the villains but the heroes. In the Old Testament, Abraham's servant was quite sure that God was behind his master's wealth, and King David prayed, 'All riches and wealth come from you.' Take this kind of teaching on its own and it suggests that the best Christians should be millionaires!

These two voices from the Bible sound discordant. In reality, however, they are both pointing us, in harmony, to the most important feature of a genuinely Christian attitude to money and possessions.

Attitudes

'Attitude' is, in fact, the key word. According to the Bible, it is not the quantity or value of the things we own that decides whether we are living rightly or wrongly. What matters above everything else is our attitude of mind to the things we possess—whether they are few or many.

Jesus exposed the root of all wrong attitudes. 'No one can be a slave to two masters,' he said. 'You cannot serve both God and money.' This is the light in which we are meant to see his instruction to the rich young man to sell everything he had. Here was a wealthy person who had allowed his possessions to

possess him. Jesus' aim was to make him realize that money had put bars across the windows of his life, and then to help him escape from his self-made prison.

Money makes a good servant but a bad master. This is the conviction that lies at the heart of Christian teaching about money and possessions. Paul captured its spirit exactly when he wrote to Timothy, 'The love of money (not money itself) is a source of all kinds of evil.' And again it is Jesus who spells out the consequences of money-mastery most clearly. At the *personal* level, he said, the result of putting money first in life will be either a permanent anxiety complex (shading into envy of those who have more) or a complacently false sense of security (forgetting that we can't take it with us when we go). At the *relationships* level, preoccupation with possessions will blind us to the needs of others. (How can you afford to contribute to famine relief when you have to extend the garage to fit the new car?). And at the *spiritual* level, making an idol out of money will cut our lines of communication with God.

The Marxist analysis

Christians are not, of course, the only people who sound these warning notes. Karl Marx was particularly vocal in condemning the tyranny of a money-centred lifestyle. 'Alienation' was his favourite word to describe the way the money bug makes people downgrade their work as an unfortunately necessary means to a pay-packet, and drives them to compete selfishly with their neighbours for the latest status symbols.

The fault, as Marx saw it, lay more in the structures of the money system than in human nature. He identified capitalism as the chief culprit. There is no hope for individual men and women, he believed, so long as they live under a system which makes them slaves to consumption and competition. They are totally at the mercy of subtle advertising techniques which persuade them to buy consumer products with built-in obsolescence

that they don't really want, and to increase their own little pile of material possessions with little or no thought for anyone else's. Only when the capitalist system is smashed, and private ownership replaced by communism, will ordinary men and women revert to their natural state—which is to cooperate in a harmony of unselfish care for one another.

Stewardship

There is a great deal in Marx' analysis of the money-centred life that rings loud bells in Christian ears. It would certainly be hard to defend out-and-out capitalism from the New Testament. In so far as it breeds selfishness and greed, the capitalist way of life would no doubt have attracted Jesus' own criticism. But Marx' solution is far too simple. It relies on a highly optimistic view of human nature. As a medicine for self-centred attitudes deeply embedded in our personalities, the Marxist offers us a set of new social structures. That, to the Christian, is rather like offering a dose of cough mixture to someone with lung cancer. It just doesn't get to the root of the problem. Important though social structures are in shaping people's opinions and habits (more important, perhaps, than some Christians admit), they cannot change human nature.

The Bible's antidote to materialism is a radical change of attitude, summed up in the word 'stewardship'. A steward does not own the resources he controls. In biblical language, 'the world and all that is in it belong to the Lord', and man's job is simply to manage what he holds on trust according to the Owner's instructions.

In this way the Christian ethic drives a middle path between the extremes of capitalism and Marxist socialism. The fact that some of God's resources (in the shape of money and property) are under my control doesn't give me the right to hoard or squander them selfishly. According to Jesus, God supplies enough for everyone in the world to enjoy a satisfactory standard of living. If, therefore, I consume so much myself that other people have

WRONG ATTITUDES TO MONEY

● **breed dangerous complacency:**
'Jesus told them this parable: "There was once a rich man who had land which bore good crops. He began to think to himself, 'I haven't anywhere to keep all my crops. What can I do? This is what I will do,' he told himself; 'I will tear down my barns and build bigger ones, where I will store my corn and all my other goods. Then I will say to myself, 'Lucky man! You have all the good things you need for many years. Take life easy, eat, drink and enjoy yourself!' But God said to him, 'You fool! This very night you will have to give up your life; then who will get all these things you have kept for yourself?''' And Jesus concluded, "This is how it is with those who pile up riches for themselves but are not rich in God's sight".'
Luke 12:16-21

● **destroy peace of mind:**
'"So do not start worrying: 'Where will my food come from? or my drink? or my clothes?' (These are the things the pagans are always concerned about.) Your Father in heaven knows that you need all these things. Instead, be concerned above everything else with the Kingdom of God and with what he requires of you, and he will provide you with all these other things".'
Matthew 6:31-33

● **blind to the needs of others:**
'"There was once a rich man who dressed in the most expensive clothes and lived in great luxury every day. There was also a poor man named Lazarus, covered with sores, who used to be brought to the rich man's door, hoping to eat the bits of food that fell from the rich man's table".'
Luke 16:19-21

● **choke spiritual life:**
'"The thorny ground represents the hearts of people who listen to the Good News and receive it, but all too quickly the attractions of this world, and the delights of wealth, and the search for success and the lure of attractive things come in and crowd out God's message from their hearts, so that no crop is produced".'
Mark 4:18-19

RIGHT ATTITUDES TO MONEY

● **strengthen dependence on God:**
'Command those who are rich in the things of this life not to be proud, but to place their hope, not in such an uncertain thing as riches, but in God, who generously gives us everything for our enjoyment.'
1 Timothy 6:17

● **bring contentment:**
'I have learnt to be satisfied with what I have. I know what it is to be in need and what it is to have more than enough. I have learnt this secret, so that anywhere, at any time, I am content, whether I am full or hungry, whether I have too much or too little. I have the strength to face all conditions by the power that Christ gives me.'
Philippians 4:11-13

● **nourish spiritual life:**
'Let everyone give as his heart tells him, neither grudgingly nor under compulsion, for God loves the man whose heart is in his gift. After all, God can give you everything that you need, so that you may always have sufficient both for yourselves and for giving away to other people . . . The more you are enriched by God the more scope will there be for generous giving, and your gifts, administered through us, will mean that many will thank God. For your giving does not end in meeting the wants of your fellow-Christians. It also results in an overflowing tide of thanksgiving to God. Moreover your very giving proves the reality of your faith, and that means that men thank God that you practise the gospel you profess to believe in, as well as for the actual gifts you make to them and to others'
2 Corinthians 9:7-8, 11-13

● **encourage generosity:**
'Somehow, in most difficult circumstances, their joy and the fact of being down to their last penny themselves, produced a magnificent concern for other people. I can guarantee that they were willing to give to the limit of their means, yes and beyond their means, without the slightest urging from me or anyone else. In fact they simply begged us to accept their gifts and so let them share the honour of supporting their brothers in Christ. Nor was their gift, as I must confess I had expected, a mere cash payment. Instead they made a complete dedication of themselves first to the Lord and then to us, as God's appointed ministers.'
2 Corinthians 8:2-5

less than enough, it is useless for me to plead 'I have a right to do what I like with the money I earn'. As a steward I have no such right.

But if stewardship rules out false ideas of private ownership, it is not the same thing as public ownership either. As God's steward I have full personal control over the money and property I hold in trust from him. In that restricted sense they are 'mine'. This boosts my sense of responsibility (something which communal ownership often erodes). It also heightens my respect for the money and property that have been entrusted to others. Among other things, this makes sense of the Bible's strict ban on stealing. If I find someone else's purse and spend the money in it, to protest 'It's as much my property as hers anyway' is no defence at all.

To sum up, Christian teaching on money and possessions focuses on attitudes, not amounts. A lifestyle dominated by love of money is wrong, whether the sums involved are huge or tiny. The right attitude is one of responsible stewardship. A good steward, said Jesus, is both gratefully dependent on God for what he has and happily generous in doing all he can to meet the needs of others.

5 MONEY

IS IT WRONG TO GAMBLE?

Christians today differ widely in their views of gambling. Many are implacably opposed to it. They are heirs to a long tradition, reaching right back to AD 200, when Bishop Tertullian of North Africa wrote, 'If you say you are a Christian when you are a dice-player, you say you are what you are not'. Others think that pinning an 'immoral' label on *all* gambling is an over-reaction against its excesses. Can it really be right to put the old lady who goes once a week to a Bingo session, and the man down the road who buys the occasional raffle ticket for a good cause, in the same bracket as the compulsive race-goer who steals for his betting money?

Whenever disagreements are strong and pressure-groups are vocal, it is vital to know exactly what we are talking about. Here, then, is a rather complicated—but carefully worded—definition of gambling.

Gambling is an agreement between two parties
whereby transfer of something of value
is made dependent on an uncertain event
in such a way that one party will gain and another lose.

That formula helps to clear the ground by ruling out of our consideration some things which are often loosely called 'gambles'. Tossing a coin to decide ends at the beginning of a football match, for example, is a deliberate appeal to chance but not really gambling. Chance and risk also figure largely in the minds of those who take out insurance policies, but the intention there is to protect against the risks of the unknown, not to create or embrace them deliberately. Straight-forward buying and selling on the stock market is not gambling, though speculation sometimes is.

Arguments about gambling are often confused. Take this imaginary three-sided conversation:

Person A: 'I think all gambling is wrong.'
Person B: 'But a lot of people do it for fun, don't they?'
Person C: 'And sometimes the money goes to a good cause!'

The trouble with that sort of discussion is that it takes place on three different wave-lengths at the same time. Let's try to unscramble them, taking them in reverse order.

Results

Sometimes the proceeds of gambling do go to a good cause. Charities organize raffles to augment their funds, as do quite a few churches. In some countries lotteries are held to provide money for social amenities. In the seventeenth century, London's metropolitan water supply and the first Westminster Bridge were financed by sales of lottery tickets. Those who bought them, but failed to win a prize, could at least comfort themselves with the thought that their stake-money had been put to a good use. The enormous bills for Sydney's imaginative Opera House were an embarrassment to the whole community, until they were paid off in a few days by means of a lottery.

At the personal level, though, the results of gambling are sometimes tragic. A businessman's wife told on a radio programme how, for her, gambling meant 'the lack of a husband, the lack of a home'. A famous footballer confessed to a popular newspaper,

Horse racing is a colourful and exciting spectator sport. And it is also the focus of betting on a large scale. Other forms of gambling, from the casino to the bingo hall, combine with betting to make a major industry in most countries. For many it is a harmless and exciting pastime. But for some it becomes a deadly addiction. Is gambling 'all right as long as you know when to stop'? Or does it offend against deep principles of fairness and the stewardship of money?

'I gambled my wife away.' Once gambling reaches the stage of addiction, the consequences are as devastating and predictable as those of alcoholism. And there are, of course, the social vultures who induce addiction and then feed off their victims. As one casino boss put it (explaining why he encouraged people to come along and watch games even if they didn't play), 'We have a motto that today's spectator is tomorrow's gambler.'

Motives

Why do people do it? Motives behind gambling can be very mixed. The most obvious is desire for gain. That need not be a bad incentive, any more than ambition need be selfish, but in the case of the gambler the shape it usually takes is a desire to get a big profit for little or no effort. That 'something for nothing' mentality is certainly sub-Christian, as is the love of money which gambling often induces. Jesus' warning to his disciples, 'Guard yourselves from every kind of greed', is particularly appropriate for the gambler who has made gain into his god.

But it would be unfair to accuse all gamblers of greed. The church member who buys a raffle ticket for the Repair Fund, wins the first prize, and then auctions it to make even more money for the appeal is hardly guilty of avarice. Nor is the elderly shut-in who goes off to Bingo on a Wednesday afternoon for some rare companionship. She may admit to getting a little excited if the numbers on her card put her in line for a prize, but is it wrong to 'do it for fun', as the second person in our imaginary conversation put it?

For the vast majority of participants, gambling is a pastime not an addiction. It may be their chosen antidote for a monotonous job, giving them the satisfaction of exercising gifts of skill and judgement that their work denies them. Is it wrong for a mountaineer to buy equipment for the enjoyment he gets from taking calculated risks, or for a sports fan to pay for the excitement of supporting his favourite team? Then it seems

WHAT SOME PEOPLE HAVE SAID AGAINST GAMBLING:

'If a man be willing or indifferent to lose his own money and not at all desirous to get another's, to what purpose is it that he plays for it? If he be not indifferent, then he is covetous or he is a fool.'
Bishop Jeremy Taylor; 1660

'The lottery is so radically vicious that your committee feels convinced that under no system of regulations which can be devised will it be possible for Parliament to adopt it.'
British Parliamentary Select Committee; 1808

'Gambling is essentially anti-social, and an embodiment of selfishness is the very essence of sin.'
Bishop B. F. Westcott; 1892

'Raffles and sweepstakes are often defended on the ground that the money for hospitals, for blinded soldiers, for orphan children, or whatever the good cause may be, cannot be raised in any other way; and that a raffle is merely for helping a good cause, nobody really caring whether they win or not. Obviously these two pleas cancel one another.'
Canon Peter Green; 1931

'Gambling challenges that view of life which the Christian church exists to uphold and extend. Its glorification of mere chance is a denial of the Divine Order in nature. To risk money haphazardly is to disregard the insistence of the church in every age of living faith that possessions are a trust, and that men must account to God for their use. The persistent appeal to covetousness is fundamentally opposed to the unselfishness which was taught by Jesus Christ and by the New Testament as a whole.'
Archbishop William Temple; 1942

THE BIBLE SAYS NOTHING ABOUT GAMBLING, BUT IT DOES WARN AGAINST:

● **Addiction:**
'Someone will say, "I am allowed to do anything." Yes; but not everything is good for you. I could say that I am allowed to do anything, but I am not going to let anything make me its slave.'
1 Corinthians 6:12

● **Greed:**
'Watch out and guard yourselves from every kind of greed.'
Luke 12:15

'Remember the words that the Lord Jesus himself said, "There is more happiness in giving than in receiving".'
Acts 20:35

● **Selfishness:**
'"We are allowed to do anything," so they say. That is true, but not everything is good. "We are allowed to do anything"—but not everything is helpful. No one should be looking to his own interests, but to the interests of others.'
1 Corinthians 10:23, 24

illogical to condemn the gambler who pays out a similar proportion of his wages with the same aims and motives. This is not to whitewash greed, but to avoid stereotyping all gamblers as greedy people.

Principles

The easiest solution, of course, is to take sides with the man who says, 'All gambling is wrong.' Whatever the results it may have, this man would say, and however it is motivated, it comes in that list of things that are simply wrong in themselves, and therefore best avoided.

The Bible does not put gambling in this category (in fact the Bible says nothing directly about gambling at all), but there are several Christian principles which seem to point in that direction. Two of the most important are those of *stewardship* and *order*.

As we saw in the last section, the principle of *stewardship* plays a vital part in shaping Christians' attitudes towards money and possessions. The Bible teaches us that we are trustees, not owners, of everything we have. This means that the gambler is deliberately putting at risk something that does not belong to him. He is staking God's money on the outcome of luck.

That certainly rules out *excessive* gambling, but it does not apply so obviously to the person who wagers with a carefully limited amount of stake-money. If, of course, the stewardship principal puts a ban on all leisure spending, gambling is wrong along with many other things (like buying records and going to the theatre). But the Bible says, 'God generously gives us everything for our enjoyment' and the Ten Commandments endorse the leisure principle by banning a seven-day working week. So presumably the principle of stewardship has room for *some* spending on leisure activities, which makes it unfair to blame the *disciplined* gambler for using God's money irresponsibly.

The principle of *order*, however, appears to go one step further. 'God', says the apostle Paul, 'is not a God of confusion.' And the rest of the Bible illustrates that truth. When he created the world, God made everything in an orderly way. Nothing was done haphazardly. And when he redeemed mankind, he prepared meticulously for Christ's arrival in the world. Both Old and New Testaments hammer home the point that there was nothing accidental in either the timing or the character of the first Christmas.

Now the basic principle of Christian behaviour is that men should imitate God. If, then, the God of the Bible is a God of order who leaves nothing to chance, it is hard to see how gambling—which thrives on chance—can possibly be a God-like activity, however self-disciplined the individual gambler may be.

So Christian teaching weights the scales against gambling—but perhaps not quite as heavily as some extreme anti-gamblers make out. The Bible does not apply the principle of order explicitly to outlaw all games of chance. Nor is it fair to say that all gambling is badly motivated—or, for that matter, to belittle the financial benefits some charities gain from the proceeds of lotteries. But even at the level of motives and consequences there are enough queries and doubts to persuade most Christians to avoid it altogether. Certainly the motives behind gambling are mixed enough to make any church or Christian charity hesitate before launching a fund-raising lottery, especially if they are convinced that a direct appeal for gifts would not bring in the same results. And there are enough human casualties from gambling to justify Christian support for measures designed to protect those who are most vulnerable to harm from addiction.

6 SEX

IS SEX OUTSIDE MARRIAGE WRONG?

'The customary response,' said the vicar sternly to the bridegroom in the cartoon, 'is "I do", not "I did"!'

Why did the cartoonist choose a vicar and not a registrar to get his laugh? Obviously because the church is linked in nearly everyone's mind with a hostile attitude towards sex outside marriage. Many even think of Christianity as being anti-sex and anti-pleasure in general. If you're not married, stifling your sex-drive is part of the price you have to pay for being a Christian. You are taught in church to think about God as some kind of a kill-joy, rather like the harassed mother who yells to her older children, 'Find out what the baby's doing and make him stop.'

A glance in the history books is enough to show us that the church has done plenty to earn this negative image. One piece of early Christian writing even describes sexual intercourse as 'an experiment of the serpent ... the impediment which separates from the Lord'. Not long afterwards a famous theologian castrated himself in the belief that he could serve God better without his sexual powers. And within a space of two hundred years an influential bishop wrote, 'Married people ought to blush when they consider the sort of life they live.' If Bishop Ambrose thought a married couple's sex life should cause them such embarrassment one can easily guess at his opinion of extra-marital intercourse!

The Bible's view

Before we go any further it is worth noticing how sharply this traditional, suspicious attitude towards sexual pleasure contrasts with the Bible's teaching. To hear some people talk,

Books, films, television plays, often take extramarital sex for granted. This puts pressure on young people to start their sexual experience early. How strong are the arguments for confining full sexual experience within marriage?

you would think Christians are meant to believe that God created man and then the devil came along and invented sex. According to the book of Genesis, nothing could be further from the truth. It was God himself who distinguished male from female. It was he who brought them together to be 'one flesh', and it was he who labelled everything he had made (including sexuality) very good.

The rest of the Bible echoes this positive note. The author of the Book of Proverbs, for example, writes: 'Rejoice in the wife of your youth. Let her affection fill you at all times with delight, be infatuated always with her love.' Another Old Testament book, the Song of Songs, pulsates with delight in a young couple's physical love-making. And even Ecclesiastes, whose serious calling it was to explode the 'eat, drink and be merry' myth, said 'Enjoy life with the woman you love.'

It won't have escaped the careful reader's attention, of course, that all these quotations and allusions are about sex *in marriage*. On sex *out of marriage* the tone of the Bible's teaching quickly changes from warm welcome to strict prohibition. According to the New Testament pre-marital intercourse, like adultery, is to be shut out of the Christian's life completely, even if that means running away from compromising situations or avoiding suggestive conversations.

Two modern views

Why does the Bible distinguish so clearly between sex inside and outside marriage? Before we explore the reasons and try to relate them to the very different conditions of life today, it will help to make one further important distinction.

People who have sex outside marriage today—and see nothing wrong about it—do so for a variety of reasons, but broadly speaking they fall into two main categories. First there are those who think of their sex-drive primarily as a *physical appetite*. On this view, as one psychologist has aptly put it, 'chastity is no more of a virtue than malnutrition'. A hungry man who turns his back on a good dinner is a fool, not a paragon of virtue. In the same kind of way a man (or a woman) who stifles his (or her) sexual appetite, when there are means available to satisfy it, is surely being more of an idiot than a saint.

This approach to sex fits in well with the tendency in modern advertising to picture men and women as sex-objects rather than as people. Here, too, is the main justification for prostitution. Both the prostitute and her client accept sexual intercourse as a contract, not a relationship. On the one side physical release is promised, and on the other side a fee. The 'bed event' is a meeting of two bodies, nothing more. Indeed, if the client attempted to stretch the sexual act into the beginnings of a relationship, the prostitute would probably object very strongly.

Then, second, there are those who see sexual intercourse as a *mark of close friendship*. They would fight shy of casual sex (and shudder at the thought of doing it for money), but see nothing wrong in expressing their physical affections in bed providing there was full consent and desire on both sides. They would say the right answer to the old question 'If you love me, why don't you let me?' is 'I do love you, so let's.' On this view, the difference between intercourse and foreplay (kissing and caressing) is only one of degree.

For those in this second category marriage may or may not come into the picture. Some deliberately opt for an extra-marital relationship as something better than getting married. Marriage, they feel, would spoil their love by institutionalizing it. Others look forward to wedlock as the probable goal of their relationship—but believe they should test their physical compatibility first, before they take so important a step.

Why the veto?

And where, you may be thinking, is the wrong in that? Isn't it better for someone with a strong sex drive to find release than slip into repression? And shouldn't we praise a couple who want to use sex to seal and improve their relationship, whether as an alternative to marriage or as a preparation for it?

A great deal of impatience with the traditional veto on extra-marital sex can be traced to the inadequacy of the arguments used to support it. Often, these are based on consequences. 'Don't do it,' young people are told, 'because dreadful things will happen if you do!' The implication is that the wrongness of doing it will disappear if the harmful results can be avoided. And, as we all know, many can be. The pill virtually ensures that an unwanted baby need not be started and good clinics provide powerful antibiotics to cure those unlucky enough to pick up venereal disease.

It would be wrong, of course, to pretend that all the risks have completely receded. The only totally reliable contraceptive is still the word 'No', and VD has reached epidemic proportions in some Western countries. But the fact remains that a careful couple can be almost certain of avoiding these dreadful consequences on which many of the old arguments still depend.

Against this back-cloth, it is interesting to see that the Bible does not base its case against extra-marital sex on the harm it may do. The Bible, in fact, is far more interested in what sexual intercourse is for, than in the results it may or may not have. And this is the basis on which its vetoes rest.

Apart from its obvious role in producing babies, *intercourse was made by God to strengthen relationships.* That is the message of the creation stories in the book of Genesis. God detected one inadequacy in his making of Adam—human aloneness. So Eve was created to fill that relationship vacuum, and the way in which she was made highlighted the personal intimacy 'becoming one flesh' was meant to protect and strengthen.

Exclusive commitment

Here is the Bible's answer to those

BIBLE CONTRASTS

IN MARRIAGE:

● **The Bridegroom:**
'How beautiful you are, my love! How your eyes shine with love behind your veil . . .

Your lips are like a scarlet ribbon; how lovely they are when you speak.

How beautiful you are, my love; how perfect you are!

Your love delights me, my sweetheart and bride.'

● **The Bride:**
'Promise me, women of Jerusalem, that if you find my lover, you will tell him I am weak from passion.

My love is handsome and strong; he is one in ten thousand. His face is bronzed and smooth; his hair is wavy, black as a raven.

His mouth is sweet to kiss; everything about him enchants me.

My lover is mine, and I am his.'
Song of Songs

OUT OF MARRIAGE:

'God wants you to be holy and completely free from sexual immorality.'
1 Thessalonians 4:3

'Avoid sexual immorality. Any other sin a man commits does not affect his body; but the man who is guilty of sexual immorality sins against his own body. Don't you know that your body is the temple of the Holy Spirit who lives in you and who was given to you by God?'
1 Corinthians 6:18-19

'Anyone who even looks at a woman with lust in his eye has already committed adultery with her in his heart.'
Matthew 5:28

CASUAL SEX?

'There is no such thing as casual sex, no matter how casual people are about it. The Christian assaults reality in his night out at the brothel. He uses a woman and puts her back in a closet where she can be forgotten; but the reality is that he has put away a person with whom he has done something which was meant to inseparably join them.'
Lewis Smedes

NOT READY?

'A girl plays at sex for which she is not ready, because fundamentally what she wants is love; and the boy plays at love, for which he is not ready, because what he wants is sex.'
Mary Calderone

ONE-MAN WOMAN

I am at a party. And about 2 a.m., when everybody was too tired to leave, the discussion got around to sex. We were silly enough to count how many sex partners we had had.

There were about a dozen of us, me being next to last. The answers ranged from two to hundreds. When it was almost my turn, I got a bit nervous. My turn. Do I dare reveal the truth? What will my close friends think?

"Well", I began, almost apologizing, "I've only slept with one man".

"Before your husband?" asked Karen, who was still counting.

"Including my husband. My answer is one."

"One?" They all screamed, put down wine glasses, rolled their eyes and held back laughter. The person after me never got her chance to go. My answer was so unique, so amusing, so interesting that the entire game stopped with me.

"Aren't you curious?" they asked.

No, I'm not curious because it seems to me that Karen the counter is always tearfully relating bad sexual experiences from one man to another. Let her count.

And here's the real shocker—I like being a one-man woman. I'm just fine, thank you. More than fine. Because you know what? I believe the one-man woman has more romance and candlelight dinners than all the rest of them.'
Gail Parent

who think of sex as just an appetite. The couple who go to bed with each other only because they are hungry for physical satisfaction are missing out on the whole point of intercourse. The apostle Paul takes the extreme case of the prostitute to hammer home this point: 'Don't you know that if a man joins himself to a prostitute she becomes a part of him and he becomes a part of her? For God tells us in the Scriptures that in his sight *the two become one person.*'

In other words, sexual intercourse affects us as whole people, not just as bundles of appetites in search of satisfaction. Its purpose is not merely to link up two bodies in a few minutes of physical ecstasy and relief, but to unite two partners in an ever-deepening relationship. Treating sex like famine relief is wrong, according to Christian teaching, not because it delights and satisfies but because the satisfaction and delight it brings are so pitifully partial and temporary.

Here, though, we have to pause because there are many stopping-off points between a 'monkey-and-banana' attitude to sex at one extreme, and a wedding ceremony at the other. Marriage implies an exclusive, permanent relationship. But, as we all know, affectionate relationships can exist at other levels too. So why shouldn't two people express a close friendship by going to bed—even if they are not at all sure that they want to spend the rest of their lives together?

Again, the story of creation provides the beginnings of an answer in the way it describes the purpose of sexual intercourse. In the Creator's plan, intercourse is not the appropriate expression of just *any* affectionate friendship. *It is the right seal on two people's exclusive commitment to each other for life*—in other words, on their *marriage.*

Jesus himself took up the language of Genesis to underline the very special place of marriage. It puts every other relationship in the shade, he taught, including the very closest family ties (the husband 'leaves father and mother'). It joins husband to wife so closely that separation leaves them both torn and hurt (he is 'joined to his wife'—and the Bible's word for 'join' means 'stick'). And sexual intercourse, the physical seal on that union, marks its uniqueness in an appropriately special way ('they become one').

Here, then, lies the reason behind the Bible's insistence that the right place for intercourse is in marriage alone. A kiss and a cuddle can mean 'I like you a lot'. But intercourse is a deeper kind of body language altogether. It says, on each side, 'Whatever the future holds, I am giving myself to you for the rest of my life, and the oneness we share will always be exclusive to ourselves.'

And that is the language of marriage, not of open-ended friendship.

WHAT ABOUT SAME SEX RELATIONSHIPS?

Making friends with someone of the same sex is the most natural thing in the world. Children do so in school playgrounds, teenagers in youth clubs and adults in sports teams. Men slip away from their wives to enjoy a chat over a drink with other men, while women look forward to a leisurely half-hour over a cup of coffee with their women-friends.

Inject the word 'homosexual' into a conversation, however, and the scene changes dramatically! Jokes about fairies or pansies harden into expressions of disgust and provoke equally angry reactions. Once a sexual (in the sense of a genital) dimension is added to a same-sex relationship, people divide into opposite camps. And the arguments often generate more heat than light.

It always helps in this kind of situation to clarify the issues. Let's begin, then, with an important distinction between people and their behaviour.

Homosexual people

It is easy to think of homosexuals as heterosexual people who have got into bad habits. All they need do is recognize the error of their ways and start making 'decent' and 'natural' relationships with people of the opposite sex.

Some, no doubt, fit that description exactly. They look on all sex as a toy and dabble in homosexuality out of sheer curiosity and a desire for a new experience. If they live in mono-sex institutions like a prison or the army, they may use a homosexual relationship as a stop-gap outlet for their sex drive until attractive members of the opposite sex become available.

These people, however, are in the minority among homosexuals. In fact they are not true homosexuals at all. A genuinely homosexual person is someone (male or female) who has never known what it is to be attracted to somebody of the opposite sex. He (if it is a he) feels drawn to other men in exactly the same way as his heterosexual neighbour gets excited when a pretty girl walks by.

It is about as logical to blame someone like this for his feelings as it is to blame a small boy with measles for his 'unnatural' spots. No true homosexual has asked to be the way he is. Many are bitterly ashamed and search endlessly for ways to change or suppress their sex drive. Some get married (usually disastrously) and even have children in a desperate attempt to appear normal in a heterosexual world. Only a few parade 'Gay Lib' badges—and even they often do so only as a defiant appeal for acceptance and justice.

In all discussions about homosexuality it is important to know who the people we're talking about actually are. We should also be aware that a homosexual person doesn't necessarily indulge in homosexual behaviour. Many don't.

Disguised prejudices

Homosexuality debates also get bogged down by prejudices which masquerade as moral convictions. Let's try to identify one or two of them.

First, there is *disgust*. It is easy to wrinkle your nose at things you find nauseating. Take food, for example. Some people eat things that would make other people sick, but that doesn't make it immoral for a Frenchman to enjoy his snails or an Englishman his jellied eels. In the same kind of way, a heterosexual person may find the thought of homosexual practice sickening. But his emotional reaction of disgust is not the same thing as a thought-out judgement about right and wrong.

Closely linked to disgust is *cultural conditioning*. Our ideas about sex are probably influenced more powerfully than anything else

THE BIBLE BANS HOMOSEXUAL BEHAVIOUR . . .

'No man is to have sexual relations with another man; God hates that.'
Leviticus 18:22

'Even the women pervert the natural use of their sex by unnatural acts. In the same way the men give up natural sexual relations with women and burn with passion for each other. Men do shameful things with each other, and as a result they bring upon themselves the punishment they deserve for their wrongdoing.'
Romans 1:26-27

'Don't fool yourselves. Those who live immoral lives—who are idol worshippers or adulterers or homosexuals—will have no share in God's kingdom . . . There was a time when some of you were just like that, but now your sins are washed away, and you are set apart for God, and he has accepted you because of what the Lord Jesus Christ and the Spirit of our God have done for you.'
1 Corinthians 6:9-11

. . . BUT LIFE IS FAR FROM EASY FOR HOMOSEXUAL PEOPLE

'The greatest hazard of the homosexual, and the one that leads to suicide, is their spiritual loneliness.'
W. L. Tonge

'Of course you can be preoccupied for a good deal of the time with your work, and find that it really does takes your mind off yourself. Even so you can hardly help but have some leisure; and what is to fill that? Well, a whole heap of interests, to keep your time and your

hands and your thoughts busy, yes, and your emotions too. But what then? At the end of the most exciting game, or the most enjoyable excursion, or the most sublime concert—what then? You come home to yourself again: the embers are cold in the grate, and the house is empty.'
Alex Davidson

. . . THOUGH THEY CAN BE HELPED BY REAL CHRISTIAN CARE

'The tremendous burdens of discrimination, intolerance, ridicule, guilt and lack of love that are loaded upon the backs of gay people (often by Christians) cannot be lightly dismissed. As you relate to people with gay tendencies, remember their pain . . .

'I was helped immensely by a family that practised aggressive, hospitality. They not only shared their food but their entire home. They opened their lives and provided a place of rest and refreshment when I was weary or discouraged. By practising biblical hospitality, they provided a place where my burdens could be shared and laid down. I wish other gay people could experience that kind of acceptance and love.'
Marty Hansen

by the views of those around us. Kissing someone of the same sex, for example, is a perfectly acceptable sign of friendship in London or New York if you happen to be a girl, but provocative homosexual behaviour if you're a boy. In Paris it's different—men kiss cheeks without any risk of being charged with indecency. Again, this kind of cultural change should alert us to the danger of translating our own reactions too easily into moral judgements.

Then, too, there is *caricature*. This can take several forms, ranging from the stereotyping of homosexual people on television programmes to gross exaggerations of the threats they pose to young children. Perhaps the most damaging distortion is the branding of all homosexuals as bed-hoppers. Some certainly live on one-night stands (as some heterosexuals do), but many long for a loving, lasting relationship just as keenly as heterosexual people look forward to getting married. Whatever our conclusions about homosexual behaviour, we must take care not to misrepresent those who practise it.

Right or wrong?

So what should our conclusions be? In reaction to the injustice homosexual people undoubtedly suffer, movements for 'Gay Rights' have received a great deal of sympathy and support in recent years. These have found their counterparts in pressure-groups within the churches, like the Gay Christian Movement in Britain and the Metropolitan Community Church in the United States. Their crusade is based on an appeal to love, summed up very well in this question put by a British Methodist minister, Leonard Barnett. 'Is it not flagrantly unchristian, unloving,' he asks, 'ruthlessly to deny the gay person the right to exercise, responsibly and lovingly, his capacity for love—including sexual loving?'

The Bible majors on love (as of course Jesus does), but its answer to that question is a firm 'No'. The Old Testament labels all homosexual conduct something God hates, and the New Testament explains that it affronts his will as man's Creator and King. It makes a big difference, of course, whether two homosexual people are just out for an hour's physical excitement or intend a life-long relationship of committed love, but whatever their motives the Bible's verdict is the same. If two people of the same sex have intercourse together they have done something as wrong as committing adultery.

The New Testament, in fact, makes the link with adultery explicit, and it is this that explains better than anything else why the whole Bible reacts to homosexual behaviour so negatively. As we saw in the last section on sex outside marriage, sexual intercourse is intended to be a special, exclusive seal on a committed, lifelong relationship between a man and a woman. If a husband commits adultery because he has 'fallen in love' with another woman, he has misunderstood what love and

intercourse are all about. And it is much the same with homosexual behaviour. People who indulge in it are using their sex organs in a way their Creator never intended. He is not necessarily against their relationship, but he is against the way they express it.

Practical promises

All this sounds terribly harsh. Does the Christian gospel reduce homosexuals to repressed, love-starved people who are forced to find a solace for their loneliness in religion? It is never very helpful to hold up a big sign saying STOP unless there is an arrow on it pointing to a better way.

The Bible does, in fact, record two positive, practical promises to homosexual people. The first is *power to change*. Some homo-sexuals seek and find God's power to change their whole sexual outlook. Others find their feelings do not alter, but discover new power to resist temptation. Either way, the most important thing Christianity says to homosexuals is not 'You mustn't', but 'In Christ's power, you needn't.' God is not a sadist. He never makes demands without first giving the resources to meet them. And there is a world of difference between the liberating control of God's Spirit and a desperate struggle for self-discipline.

The second of the Bible's promises to homosexual people is *potential for love.* Perhaps the most dangerous heresy around today is the suggestion that if you do not 'make love' you can never know what love is all about, and therefore never find personal fulfilment. The Christian gospel offers the same love-potential to virgins as to the sexually experienced. In fact it implies that some very sexually experienced people know far less about real love than others who have never had intercourse at all. Jesus' own example is helpful here. He never went to bed with a woman or a man. Yet he was the most perfectly fulfilled person who has ever lived, and he knew far more about love than we ever shall.

Love, of course, is meaningless without relationship. And the tragedy is that homosexuals are often made to feel as isolated as trees in a desert. 'You come home to yourself again,' confides one man, 'and brother, it's so lonely. Naturally the answer is that I need a wife, someone who will truly be my "other half". The answer is marriage. Which is out of the question.' Many homosexuals get involved in gay clubs more to find friends than to get casual sex (though even that may be accepted as a substitute for friendship). Some know they would meet rejection, not support, if they owned up to their feelings in church. Where that is true, it is Christian *hetero*sexuals who need the forgiveness first.

6 SEX

IS IT RIGHT TO CONTROL BIRTH?

'It was ten times simpler than having a tooth out.' That was the verdict of a woman who became pregnant in an unusual way. An egg had been removed from her ovary, fertilized by her husband's sperm in a dish and implanted into her womb. 'There is nothing unnatural in this,' she went on. 'He (the consultant) is helping me to create a child I would normally not have and very dearly want.'

Some of the most spectacular advances in medicine during recent years have been made in the field of birth control. Couples who long for children without success have been given new hope by the availability of artificial insemination. And contraceptive techniques, culminating in the pill, now give a very high degree of security to women who want sex without babies.

Today we tend to be so obsessed with the need to avoid unwanted babies that we forget the thousands of couples who badly want children but cannot—for one reason or another—start or sustain a pregnancy. The two problems seem completely different. In reality, however, they are the opposite sides of the same coin. Whether the aim is to help conception or to hinder it, artificial techniques are called in to control the normal processes of giving birth. And that raises crucial moral issues, especially for Christians who believe that all control over life and death belongs to God alone.

Broadly speaking, we can find some pointers to the rights and wrongs of controlling birth by asking these questions:

Is it natural?

That is a question you can ask in different ways. Certainly at the physical level both contraception and artificial insemination are deliberate attempts to stop nature taking its course. At the level of feelings, too, it is hard to think of either as a completely natural way of doing things. Some couples prefer the risk of starting an unwanted baby to wearing a condom or a cap simply because they feel an artificial device would spoil the emotional dimension of their love-making. And there can surely be nothing less intimate or alluring than the injection of sperm from a syringe on a table in a clinic.

But the moral force of this question goes much deeper than either the physical or the emotional levels. It really reaches right down to the meaning and purpose of sexual intercourse itself. Here, in fact, is the main plank in the official Roman Catholic platform against contraception. Nature teaches us, says the Pope's encyclical on birth control, that sexual intercourse has two goals. One is to strengthen the love-bond between husband and wife, and the other is to start new life. Those two aims must never be separated. But contraception encourages love-making without procreation, and artificial insemination opens up the way to procreation without love-making. Both are therefore wrong, in the eyes of the Roman Church, because they are unnatural.

Many Christians (including some Roman Catholics) fail to find this argument convincing, especially as it affects contraception. Providing a husband and wife do not shut the door completely on having a family (without some excellent over-riding reason), it is hard to see why it should be 'unnatural' (in the broadest sense) for them to use artificial aids to stop conception *on particular occasions*.

The same kind of reply can be made to those who would rule out all methods of assisting conception by artificial means. If it is 'natural' for a husband and wife with a normal sex life to have children, why should it be wrong to help them start a baby by using modern medical aids?

This leads on to our next main question.

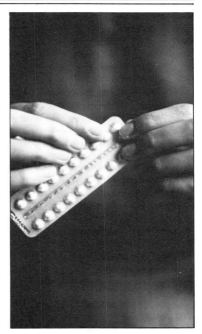

The pill makes birth control so easy today. Is its arrival all gain? Or are there any moral objections to its use?

Is it playing God?

This is a religious person's question, but many non-religious people ask it in their own way. Has modern man grown too big for his boots? Future developments of birth control techniques are particularly frightening. Sinister phrases like 'genetic engineering' and 'selective breeding' provoke panic questions. Do we really want the future of the human race shaped in the geneticist's laboratory? Test-tube babies may be fine, but what about clones?

Some Christians believe contraception is the thin end of this particular wedge. The language of 'family planning', they say, is just a symptom of human pride. It is God's prerogative to plan families, not man's. A married couple should have intercourse in the normal way and leave the results to God. If no babies arrive they should accept that as his will, instead of rushing off to the fertility clinic. And if their fertility level proves to be embarrassingly high, they should either limit intercourse to the woman's safe period or enjoy the blessings of a large family. After all, didn't God command man to 'be fruitful and multiply'? And doesn't the Bible commend the man who has his 'quiver full' of children?

Again, this is by no means a water-tight argument. The Bible verse about the 'quiver full' was aimed at people living in a half-empty world, where every new life meant another productive pair of hands. Today we live in an over-full world. In some places now every new birth is a threat to another child's life. And God's command to multiply was part of humanity's larger commission to manage the world responsibly.

In this light, contraception can be seen more as a God-given tool for managing the world's resources than as a man-made threat to God's supremacy. We know God intends man to use his skills to control and shape the pattern of nature. And we accept that principle readily enough when we inoculate babies against disease, use medicines and purify drinking water. So if we find no moral difficulty in controlling infant mortality, why should we have any scruples about using similar technical know-how to control birth?

Does it encourage wrong attitudes?

Every new scientific discovery or technological development brings its abuses as well as its blessings, and the technology of birth control is no exception. The possibility of planning births may, for example, become an excuse for planning them away. A couple may avoid

WHAT PEOPLE ARE SAYING ABOUT

CONTRACEPTION

● **in favour:**
'We believe in the right of children to be wanted . . . therefore we favour the principle of voluntary child-bearing, believing that it safeguards the well-being of family and society.'
A Congregational Church statement

● **against:**
'The Church, calling men back to the observance of the norms of the natural law, as interpreted by her constant doctrine, teaches that each and every marriage act must remain open to the transmission of life.'
Humanae Vitae, the papal encyclical on birth control

● **in favour:**
'The intimate physical union of intercourse is meant to be an expression of, and a means of enriching the unique relationship of marriage; it is the cement which bonds husband and wife into "one flesh". The release of tensions and the deepening of love spill over to enrich the relationship between parents and their children. Now if this coming together is to fulfil these aims it must be free from the tensions which are inevitable if an unacceptable pregnancy is being risked.'
Rex Gardner, gynaecologist and minister of the United Free Church of Scotland

● **against:**
'It is to be feared that the man, growing used to the employment of anti-conceptive practices, may finally lose respect for the woman and, no longer caring for her physical and psychological equilibrium, may come to the point of considering her as a mere instrument of selfish enjoyment, and no longer as his respected and beloved companion.'
Humanae Vitae

ARTIFICIAL INSEMINATION BY HUSBAND

● **in favour:**
'As far as I am concerned there is no difference in creating a baby this way. The clinical side of it is something you don't think about. It is still a husband and wife working together to create a child, only with a little help from the doctors.'
Husband of a woman pregnant after 'in vitro' fertilization

● **against:**
'Many would feel considerable reluctance on aesthetic grounds to such an obviously "clinical" procedure, or might even regard it as repugnant to their innate sense of the dignity of man . . . Again, a marriage may be all that God intends it to be without the advent of children—and the fact that they do not come may well be accepted, in some cases, as an indication of the divine will.'
Sir Norman Anderson, formerly Director of the Institute of Advanced Legal Studies at London University

ARTIFICIAL INSEMINATION BY DONOR

● **in favour:**
'Our service will open up a whole new era. We are expecting thousands of enquiries from women who cannot conceive because of their husbands. We would not necessarily turn away an unmarried woman who wants to have a baby by AID and the same would apply to lesbian couples.'
Spokeswoman for the British Pregnancy Advisory Service, at the launching of a nationwide AID scheme

● **against:**
'What degree of human degeneration or what degree of primitive underdevelopment in instincts and ideas is required to play the role of an anonymous spermator (sperm donor)? Here again every analogy with blood donation deserts us. The parallel with prostitution does, however, suggest itself (though, of course, only with respect to this one aspect of the semen donor). For here, too, the sex process becomes anonymous and impersonal.'
Helmut Thielicke, German Lutheran theologian

having children for selfish reasons, to preserve their standard of living, perhaps, or to protect their career prospects. And the availability of contraceptives (especially to the unmarried) may encourage a sub-human approach to sexual intercourse which treats it more as a release for animal instincts than as a seal on a committed relationship. These attitudes would find their way to the surface anyway, of course. But contraception does remove some of the traditional controls.

It is good rule never to let abuse of a thing obscure its value. Beside the wrong attitudes contraception allows one could set quite a long list of good attitudes it encourages. A married couple may express love for their family, for example, by using a chosen method of birth control to space their children for the maximum benefit of all. A sensible use of contraceptives will also allow them to plan the size of their family more effectively than they otherwise could, and in that way make a small, personal contribution towards easing world crises caused by the population explosion. Contraception itself, like atomic power, is neutral. It depends on those who use it whether it is made to serve good or bad ends.

At the other end of the spectrum, similar arguments can be used to justify artificial insemination. Certainly, the use of AIH (the 'H' standing for husband) comes out very well, morally speaking, when the attitudes of husband and wife are the standard by which it is judged. A couple may desire a child to express and extend their love-bond, or for some other excellent reason. If tests show that neither partner is completely sterile, the use of a syringe—or even 'in vitro' (out of the womb) fertilization—may give them the baby they so rightly want. In such cases, the availability of medical aids does not call for an embarrassed moral cover-up. In Christian terms, it should spark off open, joyful thanksgiving to God.

Here, however, AIH contrasts sharply with AID (where 'D' stands for an anonymous donor). If a husband and wife decide to start a baby by AID their own motives may be blameless, but they cannot turn a blind eye to the attitude of the donor. He has been paid for his contribution—otherwise, presumably, he would not have made it. Sperm banks depend on the profit motive for their assets. And any sex act (in this case masturbation) which is undertaken impersonally for money is highly questionable on moral grounds.

Does it threaten relationships?

An argument sometimes used to persuade a husband and wife to avoid artificial methods of birth control is that contraceptives will spoil the intimacy of their marriage relationship. Because the possibility of starting a baby is built into the heart of the sex act (the argument goes), intercourse will not be completely fulfilling if that possibility is frustrated.

All Christians believe that one of the main purposes of sexual intercourse is to deepen a married couple's relationship, so this argument would carry great weight in Christian circles if it could be proved. The evidence, however, points in the other direction. By removing the fear of starting an unwanted baby, contraceptives allow a couple more freedom, not less, to enjoy their physical intimacy. That is certainly the conclusion Rex and Elizabeth Gardner, a husband-and-wife gynaecological team, have reached after many years spent dealing with marriage problems. 'In our clinical experience,' they write, 'we have found that any other course leads to tensions and frustrations in the marriage, tensions which spill over adversely to affect the children.'

Again, however, this question raises serious doubts about the morality of AID. It is going too far to say that receiving an anonymous donor's sperm is an act of adultery, because the wife does not intend to be unfaithful to her husband and she has no emotional involvement with the donor. But the intrusion of a third party (the donor) can cause serious disruptions in their marriage later. The baby, when it comes, is truly the wife's but not truly the husband's. The fulfilment of her motherhood is not matched by the fulfilment of his fatherhood—in fact he may find that he sees in the child a nagging reminder of his own impotence. It is all too easy to see how this imbalance may aggravate relationships not only between 'father' and child but between husband and wife.

If other medical aids (including AIH) fail, the alternatives open to a childless couple are very limited. Adoption may be a possibility; many have found complete fulfilment in adopting a child. But in some parts of the world today queues of would-be adopters far outnumber the babies available. Inevitably some couples are disappointed, and the stronger their longing for children the more attractive the possibility of having a baby by AID may seem. Nevertheless, artificial insemination by a third-party donor raises more moral and practical problems than it solves. Most Christians would draw the line at this point in their search for children. If the route to adoption is blocked, they will look to God to fill the child-shaped gap in their lives in his own way, confident that those who approach life with that attitude never come off second-best.

HOW DO WE USE EARTH'S RESOURCES?

Not so long ago, people were very much at the mercy of their environment. If disease threatened their crops, they were forced to plant elsewhere or starve. If the rains failed, their cattle perished. If their children caught any one of a large number of infections, they died. Their freedom to control their surroundings was severely limited.

Modern technology has changed a great deal of that. Drought and sickness are still major threats, of course, but our ability to control them has increased dramatically. We can irrigate deserts, control diseases, develop new strains of cereal and travel at great speed over vast distances. In so many different ways we have learned how to manipulate the world around us. And forecasts of new discoveries from the research laboratories promise to make our control even greater.

But this new freedom has brought some frightening problems with it. As Dr Edmund Leach writes, 'Science offers us total mastery over our environment, yet instead of rejoicing we are deeply afraid. Why should this be?' The title of his book, *Runaway World*, suggests the answer. When man faces the world with the power-tools of technology in his hand, he is like a learner driver sitting behind the wheel of a powerful car that he cannot fully control. He *can* drive at over 100 m.p.h.—but *should* he? We are free to manipulate our environment, but ought we to put restraints on our freedom? *Should* technological man do everything that he *can* do?

The crisis of the environment

There are many indications that our human mastery of our environment is precariously poised. Pollution, for example, is an embarrassing and increasingly dangerous side-effect of progress. When a capital city's traffic police are required to inhale pure oxygen after they have come off duty, and when large areas of the Mediterranean and Baltic seas can no longer sustain marine life because of the high level of sewage and chemical waste in their waters, it is doubtful where the balance of freedom lies. The disposal of nuclear waste from power stations raises even harder questions. In his period of office as Secretary-General of the United Nations Organization, U Thant warned, 'There is arising a crisis of world-wide proportions—the crisis of the human environment. It is becoming apparent that, if current trends continue, the future of life on earth could be endangered.'

World hunger is another crisis which scientific progress has heightened. The availability of better medicine has cut the mortality rate so effectively that the world's population figures have exploded. It is reliably estimated that by the end of this century there will be more people alive (barring nuclear catastrophe) than the total of all those who have lived and died up to that point in world history. Food resources are limited. Even today, United Nations estimates put the number of severely under-nourished people at about five hundred million. And all the indications are that the problem will get worse, not better, as the years go by.

Man as manager

With the growth of these threats to the stability of the environment, there are those who would gladly put the clock back, if they could, to the time when it was possible to live the 'simple life' without the complications of things like split atoms, insecticides and internal combustion engines. Christians, however, do not subscribe to that view. According to the Bible, God's very first command to man was to 'have dominion' over the rest of creation. In other words, man is manager of the world by divine appointment. The power he exercises is not stolen from his Creator but deliberately delegated by him.

Here is all the justification the Christian needs to harness natural resources and to press forward with scientific research and technological development. The 'back to nature' cry may sound very high-minded and spiritual, but in biblical terms it is an evasion of human responsibility. Jesus told one of his best-known stories, the parable of the talents, to show how those who fail to use their God-given resources really deserve condemnation, not praise.

Bad management

In the light of the Bible's positive view of progress, it comes as no surprise to read in the history books how modern science grew up in Christian Europe. But that fact can cut both ways. Some modern historians trace the faults, as well as the benefits, of technological progress to the teaching of the Bible. Lynn White, Professor of History at the University of California, went so far as to claim that 'present science and technology is tinctured with orthodox Christian arrogance'. In his opinion, all the blame for humanity's environmental problems —the destruction of nature and the disregard for the world's future— should be laid squarely at Christianity's door.

When it comes to selfish exploitation of natural resources, Christian people are no less to blame than others. But they cannot lay the blame on the Bible's teaching. According to the book of Genesis, God told humanity to manage creation, not to exploit it. It is a manager's duty to conserve the resources entrusted to him, not to squander them carelessly. Restraint and conservation,

Ugly and cramped conditions in many cities reduce the quality of life for millions of people. To feed the cities and fuel their industries requires intensive exploitation of countryside, forests and seas. How far are we free to risk exhausting earth's resources to sustain a particular type of urban civilization?

CHRISTIAN COMMENT ON THE ENVIRONMENT CRISIS

'When I look at the sky, which you have made, at the moon and the stars, which you set in their places—what is man, that you think of him; mere man, that you care for him? Yet . . . you appointed him ruler over everything you made; you placed him over all creation.'
Psalm 8:3-6

'Until men come to believe in their hearts that all life is held in trust from God, there can be no valid ethical reason why we should owe a debt to posterity.'
Hugh Montefiore, Bishop of Birmingham

'The Conference urges all Christians, in obedience to the doctrine of creation, to take all possible action to ensure man's responsible stewardship over nature; in particular in his relationship with animals, and with regard to the conservation of the soil, and the prevention of pollution of the air, soil and ocean.'
Resolution 6 of the Lambeth Conference, 1968

'These are the two factors that lead to the destruction of our environment: money and time—or, to say it another way, greed and hate.'
Francis Schaeffer

'The Bible gives no hint of a niggardly provision that may run out. The emphasis is rather on the abundance of the creation. We would not therefore expect to find that world shortages of resources are the source of international inequality. Man may waste resources, but properly used there should be enough for all.'
Donald Hay

'In a world where hundreds of millions confront absolute poverty, those of us who enjoy relative abundance must learn to live more simply.'
Ronald Sider

'Since you have plenty at this time, it is only fair that you should help those who are in need. Then, when you are in need and they have plenty, they will help you. In this way both are treated equally. As the Scripture says, "The one who gathered much did not have too much, and the one who gathered little did not have too little".'
2 Corinthians 8:14-15

therefore, are as much characteristics of a genuinely Christian attitude to the environment as progress and development. Campaigns to limit the damaging effects of pollution, to recycle packaging materials and to distribute food stocks more fairly all deserve—and usually get—wholehearted Christian support.

When the Christian looks at environmental problems, what he sees is bad management. And behind the symptoms of bad management he diagnoses human greed and selfishness, not a breakdown in technology.

A great deal of the world's hunger problem, for example, stems from unfair distribution of food and fertilizers. It may be that agricultural technology will not be able to keep pace with the rise in the world's population for ever, but at present the evidence suggests that no one *need* starve. The Director-General of the United Nations

Food and Agricultural Organization said a few years ago, 'I would like to state firmly that the FAO has no statistical evidence suggesting that the world is proving incapable of feeding a rising population.' The heart of the food problem, in the opinion of many experts, lies in the fact that one in three Americans, and one in five Britons, suffer from obesity while Asians and Africans starve. In other words, the real culprit is not shortage of resources but selfish distribution.

Selfishness is behind a great deal of waste and pollution, too. It has been calculated, for example, that ten million metric tons of seafood is wasted annually by fishermen who specialize in one particular kind of catch and discard everything else. A scaled-down version of the same problem occurs regularly in the River Rhine. In 1969 forty million fish died in its polluted waters, and all because each of the countries

through which the river passes discharged poisonous effluent at their downstream borders. Commenting on this, a British government minister wrote, 'Human nature and organized human cupidity are such that even so simple a thing cannot be regulated.'

The problems of the environment cannot all be blamed on human nature, though. Industrial expansion inevitably causes some degree of pollution and better medicine is bound to mean that there are more people in the world to feed. Technology is already coming up with some of the solutions to the problems it has created. There are delicate economic and political problems to sort out as well. But in the Christian's view the main culprit is human selfishness, and the most powerful remedy is the neighbour-love that Jesus taught and lived out.

Neighbour-love

When Jesus told the parable of the Good Samaritan, his aim was to make his listeners broaden their love horizons. Even the unknown stranger in the story came within the range of Christian neighbour-love because of his need. Applied to the problems of today's world, that love standard has both personal and political consequences. Among other things, it means that Christians in the affluent North will never stop pressing their politicians to redress the balance of world consumption, even if increased aid results in some economic disadvantage to themselves. After all, the Third World families that go to bed hungry are just as much their neighbours as their friends down the road. So too are the men and women of future generations—which means that moves to conserve natural resources will always have the support of those who take Christ's neighbour-love teaching seriously.

At the personal level, frustration can easily take over in the face of the enormity of the world's problems. But personal example is still a powerful advertisement for love. And so Christians will see concern for conservation and famine relief having implications for themselves as well as for governments. They will want to simplify their own lifestyles. As Mother Teresa said to Malcolm Muggeridge, 'We ourselves feel that what we are doing is just a drop in the ocean. But if that drop was not in the ocean I think the ocean would be less because of that missing drop.'

According to the Bible, the first man lost his freedom when he refused to obey God's minimal restraints on his lifestyle. Christians believe that selfish, unrestrained use of natural resources today is a symptom of the same human disease. The antidote is Christ's version of neighbour-love, with the restraints it imposes on selfishness, applied at both the personal and social levels of life. That way lies true freedom.

7 FREEDOM

ARE DIVORCE AND REMARRIAGE RIGHT?

'Marriage,' said a recent church report, 'can be a foretaste of heaven or an anticipation of hell.' It would be hard to quarrel with that verdict. Some couples find everything in their married lives that they could possibly have wished for on their wedding day. Their happiness together grows as the years slip by (much too quickly), and they gain strength as they support each other through life's crises.

But for others marriage is anything but a heavenly experience. Wedding-day hopes are soon dashed. Somehow, husband and wife bring out the very worst in each other, rather than the best. Instead of ending in the warmth of 'kiss and make up', their quarrels either escalate into violence or simmer on in long periods of tight-lipped sulkiness. Communication breaks down entirely. Just being together becomes hell.

Why do marriages go sour? The reasons are many and complex. Personal failures certainly play their part, but it is usually unjust to distinguish between 'innocent' and 'guilty' parties. Breakdown situations are rarely as clear-cut as that. There may be some basic incompatibility which only comes to light after several months or even years of married life. Unseen social pressures are at work too, cracking open relationships that are already brittle. And the possibility of quick, simple divorce makes it easier to give up when things get difficult.

Whatever the reasons in individual cases, the statistics show how precariously the survival of modern marriage is balanced. In an average year in England and Wales, one established relationship ends in divorce for every three new marriages begun. The proportion of breakdowns is even higher in the United States. Naturally, critical questions are being asked more and more often about the wisdom of getting married at all.

The questions, in fact, come in two kinds. Both are dressed up as cries for freedom.

Should marriage be abolished?

Some would argue that the disadvantages of marriage outweigh its benefits. For one thing, getting married requires a couple to take life-long vows when their ability to live together has hardly been tested. To declare a man and a woman 'one flesh' in a couple of sentences is treating their relationship like instant coffee! Even if everything works out well, it is surely more healthy for them to grow in their love freely, without the artificial props of a social institution which expects them to stay together whether they like it or not. And if the arrangement proves to be a disaster, those props become the iron bars of a prison cell, which must be painfully bent and broken in the divorce court before husband and wife can regain their freedom as individuals.

Against this, the arguments in favour of marriage can be summed up in the one word *stability*. Most couples who decide to get married genuinely want a stable relationship. They don't say 'till death us do part' with their tongues in their cheeks. Both partners are looking for emotional security. *He* wants to find someone who will not leave him as soon as she finds out what he is really like; *she* longs for a partner who will not desert her in those bad moments when sickness or depression rob her of her attractiveness. There is genuine freedom in such reliability. As one young wife put it in a newspaper article, 'I don't have to worry if he's ever going to phone me again, or that I didn't turn him on or if there will ever be a next time.'

The rewards of a stable relationship are particularly great in times like our own when so much else is unpredictable. But this kind of relationship is not at all easy to

GOD'S IDEAL

'A man leaves his father and mother and is united with his wife, and they become one.'
Genesis 2:24

'Man must not separate, then, what God has joined together.'
Mark 10:9

'A married woman . . . is bound by the law to her husband as long as he lives; but if he dies, then she is free from the law that bound her to him.'
Romans 7:2

'"I hate divorce," says the Lord God of Israel. "I hate it when one of you does such a cruel thing to his wife. Make sure that you do not break your promise to be faithful to your wife".'
Malachi 2:16

GOD'S CONCESSION

'Suppose a man marries a woman and later decides that he doesn't want her, because he finds that *she is guilty of some shameful conduct.* So he writes out divorce papers, gives them to her, and sends her away from his home.'
Deuteronomy 24:1

'Jesus replied, "Moses permitted you to divorce your wives because your hearts were hard".'
Matthew 19:8

'Jesus said, "I tell you that anyone who divorces his wife, *Except for marital unfaithfulness,* and marries another commits adultery".'
Matthew 19:9

'If any brother has a wife who is not a believer and she is willing to live with him, he must not divorce her. And if a woman has a husband who is not a believer and he is willing to live with her, she must not divorce him . . . But *if the unbeliever leaves,* let him do so. *A believing man or woman is not bound* in such circumstances.'
1 Corinthians 7:12, 13, 15

sustain. In fact it is at its most vulnerable in its earliest days. Honeymoons can be major disasters, and in that first year or two the most trivial things can cause massive disruptions. No one pretends that a marriage certificate will automatically steer a couple through all their problems, but it does at least provide some kind of safety-net when their relationship threatens to fall apart. In its way it is the equivalent of a birth certificate, which does not guarantee the child's health but does at least protect it from destruction when its parents would not be sorry to see the back of it. To call that kind of restraint a 'loss of freedom' is nonsense.

Sometimes the media suggest that marriage is doomed, an outdated museum-piece, but recent statistics prove exactly the opposite. A sociologist writing in the magazine *New Society* describes 'the growing popularity of marriage amongst young people' as 'one of the most significant features of modern Britain'. And, strangely enough, it is the divorcees who provide marriage with its most impressive recommendation. Despite going through the pain of breakdown themselves, three out of every four choose to marry again. If marriage is a prison, there are long queues for accommodation in its cells.

But this takes us on to the other big question:

Should divorce and re-marriage be made easier?

If the stability which marriage brings is as precious as I have suggested, easy divorce is a menace. When it is simpler to dodge your problems than to face them, the temptation to opt out becomes irresistible. Nowadays, the British law allows divorce-by-post. This means British married couples have less reason to fight through their bad patches now than before, and therefore less incentive to grow together as they deal with the stress-points in their relationships.

But that, of course, is only half

the story. While some couples find new strength in working hard at reconciliation, others simply grow further apart. If children are involved (and they usually are) it may be worse for them to live in the tension of a divided home than to grow up in the care of one parent. In cases like that, isn't it better to give the dead marriage a decent burial without causing unnecessary, additional distress to those involved?

The churches find themselves in a dilemma at this point. Some take a very strict line, refusing to recognize any second unions in an effort to protect the values of marriage. Others welcome divorcees and conduct their re-marriage services willingly in a desire to give them the extra spiritual support they need. A few, like the American Methodist Church, even offer a special service for the Dissolution of a Marriage as a counterbalance to the wedding service.

What does the Bible say?

Many Christians who take the stricter view believe that divorce and re-marriage are not only wrong but impossible in God's sight. When Jesus said, 'Man must not separate what God has joined together,' he was simply stating a fact of life in plain language. As far as God is concerned, it is a case of 'once married, always married'. It is God who ties all marriage bonds (including the non-church ones), and no human divorce court has the power to undo the knots. When they try, it is a bit like the British Parliament solemnly declaring that London is the capital of America.

If this is a true reflection of Jesus' teaching it settles the whole question for Christians. All divorce, not just easy divorce, is wrong.

But Jesus did not quite say that. He was certainly very strict in upholding the ideal of life-long marriage—so much so that on one occasion his disciples gasped, 'If this is how it is between a man and his wife, it is better not to marry!' Nor did he spare the feelings of re-married divorcees when he bluntly declared, 'Any man who divorces

Despite all the pressures on marriage in the West today, getting married is still a very popular thing to do. The desire for a lifelong partnership is still strong in many couples.

his wife commits adultery if he marries some other woman.' But he did add one important 'except' which has puzzled and embarrassed those who claim his support for a complete ban on divorce and re-marriage. 'Except,' he said, 'for sexual unfaithfulness.'

Why did he include that exception? Well, Jesus was being faithful to the Old Testament in softening the rigidity of his pro-marriage teaching by including a concession to what he called 'hardness of heart'. And a few years later Paul accurately reflected the balance of Jesus' approach, first by firmly underlining God's ideal ('a wife must not leave her husband; but if she does, she must remain single or else be reconciled to her husband; and a husband must not divorce his wife'), and then by adding a concession of his own. All three 'excepts' cover those extreme cases where reconciliation is likely to prove least possible. In Old Testament times, the divorce decree was a wife's protection from her husband's cruelty. Jesus allowed sexual infidelity as a proper ground

for making a new start. And Paul applied the same principle to cases of desertion by husbands or wives who did not share their partners' Christian faith.

Here, then, we have the sign-post we need to point us towards a Christian answer. The whole Bible is firm in its insistence that marriage should be for life. Only then will its full values be realized. This is God's ideal. As such, the marriage bond is worth any amount of effort to preserve when it is threatened by personal failure or pressures from outside. If it fails, God's heart breaks as well as the husband's and wife's. As one of the Old Testament prophets said, putting words into God's mouth, '"I hate divorce", says the Lord.'

In a perfect world there would be no divorce at all. But we live in a world where human failures and mistakes poison all relationships, including marriage. Sometimes things get so bad that staying together becomes the worst of all possible alternatives. In the end it is a straight choice between the frying pan and the fire. In extreme situations like that, *and as a last resort when all else has failed*, Jesus did not shut the door on the possibility of both divorce and re-marriage. And the fact that he made such a concession justifies the church in sparing no effort to support those who are genuinely seeking a new start in his strength.

7 FREEDOM

IS THERE A PLACE FOR CENSORSHIP?

'An audience has the right to choose to see perversion if it wants to. Censorship is undemocratic.' So said a famous film producer when he was challenged about the screening of controversial sex and violence scenes in his latest movie. And many people would agree with him, including some who would not be seen dead in any cinema showing that particular film.

Freedom is a precious demo-cratic right. One of the things we guard most jealously is the individual's liberty to form and express his own opinions. Hence our deep suspicions whenever powerful people try to 'improve' us by banning plays, films, newspaper articles or television programmes that we might or might not want to see. There is a streak of obstinacy in most of us, anyway, which rebels strongly when the law is called in as a bureaucratic nanny to stop us enjoying ourselves, especially if it interferes in our private lives. If a notice says 'Keep off the grass', we want to walk on it. If the sale of a book is banned, we'll search for ways to get a copy.

What kind of freedom?

Freedom is a Christian value too. The kind of liberty the New Testament preaches has dimensions which take it right out of the censorship debate, but in his own terms Jesus Christ meant his people to be free. 'If the Son makes you free,' he said, 'you will be really free.'

Nevertheless, Jesus himself recognized the place of checks on personal liberty. And modern democracy does the same. Clean Air Acts are an accepted censorship of the atmosphere, for example, restraining individuals who want to make so much smoke that others cannot breathe freely. Freedom of speech is restricted by libel laws. And in the realm of social morality, we see no clash between democratic principles and laws designed to stop racial discrimination.

In recent years there have been signs of a growing conviction that people's minds can be poisoned just as fatally as their bodies. Skilfully directed propaganda can erode personal values and induce anti-social behaviour. So a case for censorship may be made out on the grounds of preserving mental health. Though the law can never make people moral, it can at least protect the moral values that most people respect, by fencing off the more obvious attacks upon them.

That, of course, makes several assumptions. For one thing, it takes for granted that what we hear and see really does influence the way we behave. And, even more important, it assumes that a list can be made of moral values and standards that the majority want to see preserved. We must explore further in both those areas. But first, some definitions.

What is censorship?

There are two kinds of censorship which cause little argument, the first because it is obvious and the second because (failing a major shake-up in social structures) it is inevitable. Anyone can exercise *personal* censorship by walking past a cinema, by turning off a TV set, or by refusing to buy a girlie magazine with the daily newspaper. And in a competitive economy *commercial* censorship will always be with us. Whether we like it or not, big business freezes out plays, films and magazines that don't pay, and strongly encourages those that do.

The main controversy centres on *reference* censorship—that is, the legal requirement to submit material to some recognized authority for checking, either before or after it is made available to the general public. There is very little pre-censorship of this kind left on the British statute-book, though customs officials have considerable powers to destroy any indecent or

THE POWER OF PORNOGRAPHY

'For about ten years I had been hooked on pornographic magazines which I bought and kept locked away in a cupboard . . . For years I had been trying to throw these papers away but couldn't bring myself to do it . . . Addiction to pornography is like a cancer of the mind.'
A doctor

'I have treated pornography addicts and find that their experience follows much the same pattern as occult involvement. Initially a person's interest is caught; then by stages he is fascinated, controlled and finally possessed. The really ill people appear to be taken over and lose all control.'
A consultant psychiatrist

'When all is said and done, pornography and violence in the media are only symptoms of a much more widespread disease, namely a general loss of values, Christian, moral or social . . . encouraged by the general permissiveness which has now engulfed both the law-makers and the law-enforcers.'
A psychologist

THE IMPORTANCE OF THE MIND

'Anyone who looks at a woman lustfully has already committed adultery with her in his heart.'
Matthew 5:28

'It is what comes out of a person that makes him unclean. For from the inside, from a person's heart, come the evil ideas which lead him to do immoral things, to rob, kill, commit adultery, be greedy, and do all sorts of evil things; deceit, indecency, jealousy, slander, pride, and folly—all these evil things come from inside a person and make him unclean.'
Mark 7:20-23

'Do not conform yourselves to the standards of this world, but let God transform you inwardly by a complete change of your mind.'
Romans 12:2

'Fill your minds with those things that are good and that deserve praise: things that are true, noble, right, pure, lovely, and honourable.'
Philippians 4:8

obscene articles they find in the process of being imported. On the post-censorship side, the Obscene Publications Act of 1964 has captured most of the headlines in Britain, mainly because it is so hard to enforce. The word 'obscenity' itself is very difficult to pin down. The law takes it to mean 'tending to deprave or corrupt', which in effect covers the violent and the pornographic. Those are certainly the pro-censorship lobby's main targets.

The effects of obscenity

Some claim that pornography, in particular, has no harmful effects at all on its consumers. A decade ago two major bodies, the Arts Council Working Party in the United Kingdom and a Presidential Commission in America, came to that negative conclusion after

carefully studying the evidence available to them. Positively, some therapists believe that blue films and books showing explicit sex acts can have beneficial results in individual cases. Lonely people find sexual release in such things, it is claimed, and some potentially dangerous people may use them to fantasize the anti-social things they might otherwise do. Evidence from Denmark is sometimes quoted to show that the rate of sex-linked crime drops when laws against pornography are relaxed.

The Scandinavian experiment is far from conclusive, however. It is true that the number of sexual offences in Denmark has dropped since pornography was legalized in 1967, but the fall is due largely—perhaps completely—to the fact that other changes in the law at about the same time removed no less than eleven different categories of crime from the statute book. There are now fewer offences against minors in Denmark—but only because the upper age limit for a 'minor' has been reduced from seventeen to thirteen! The figures for rape have actually gone up.

There is, in fact, plenty to suggest that social harm does follow the removal of restraints on obscene literature. Two of the more lurid homicide cases in Britain's recent past, the trials of the Moors murderers and of the Cambridge rapist, show how a straight line can be drawn from minds stuffed with sadism and pornography to fearful atrocities. At the end of another less-publicized case, the judge commented, 'It is often said that pornography really does not cause any evil results. On the evidence of this case, but for the literature this matter would never have arisen.'

Some people, of course, are more vulnerable to serious harm than others. Children are particularly at risk, and it is hard to see any excuse for film-makers who use eleven-year-olds in explicit sex films—or, indeed, for newsagents who display soft porn next to comics on their shelves. Most adults who pay to read pornography undoubtedly lead blameless lives (especially if they have a strong sense of humour!). But even so, Christian misgivings do not disappear.

Jesus was even more concerned with inward attitudes than he was with outward behaviour, and it is at this 'sub-action' level that obscenity has its most insidious effects. For one thing, it can deaden sensitivity to right and wrong. The New Testament talks about man's moral sense being anaesthetized through continual exposure to wrong-doing, and it would be strange if something very similar did not happen to minds deliberately opened wide to sadism and violence on and off the television screen. As one non-churchgoing journalist put it, 'I don't think that my children when they grow up are going to be particularly shocked if they see someone lying with bloodstains in the gutter, because they've seen it so many times on TV.'

Moral values

Christians would want to add that exposure to pornography erodes important moral values. It degrades women by treating them as sex-objects instead of people. It devalues sexuality by stripping away the dimensions of commitment and relationship. And it deliberately induces the kind of lust that Jesus condemned as mental adultery.

Here, of course, we have to move with caution. In a democratic society a minority group has no right to impose it values on others, even if it finds the political power to do so. British society has been called 'post-Christian', in the sense that only a minority of people admit to having Christian faith by going to church regularly. Therefore it is arguably wrong for Christians to expect their standards and values to receive special protection from the law.

The fact remains, though, that pornography does deeply offend the majority of people, whether or not they are church-goers. In a recent survey conducted by Gallup Poll, two-thirds of those questioned expressed the belief that sex is a private matter and should never be publicly displayed, filmed, or staged for money or for entertainment. Nearly as many agreed that pornography degrades women by representing them as sex objects for male use.

There is no reason why findings like these should surprise the Christian public. They simply provide contemporary evidence for what the New Testament calls 'God's law written on man's heart'. In other words, the 'gut reaction' which makes most people want to preserve the values that Jesus taught, whatever their personal beliefs, reflects the way they are made. It is all part of what it means to be human.

The same Gallup Poll showed a 70 per cent majority in favour of some censorship of plays and films. Bearing in mind the effects obscene material can have on attitudes as well as on behaviour, and the general desire to preserve moral values, the case for restraints of this kind seems overwhelmingly strong. But censorship alone can never satisfy the positive demands of the Christian gospel. Christians should be even more vigorous in promoting and reinforcing the good (the kind of things Paul summed up as 'true, noble, right, pure, lovely and honourable') than they are in exposing and condemning the bad.

7 FREEDOM

SHOULD ADVERTISING BE CURBED?

Advertisements come in all shapes and sizes. The menu in the restaurant window, the notice in the local paper and the TV commercial are all advertising something. Their purpose is twofold: first to *inform*, and then to *persuade*. Just providing the information is seldom enough by itself. On a hot afternoon, for example, a notice in a shop window saying 'Ice Cream' may be sufficient to bring the customers in, but if the supermarket next door is selling ice cream, too, the shopkeeper will have to find clever ways of persuading passers-by that his brand is better.

Christians should have no problems with these basic principles of advertising. After all, Jesus commanded his disciples to be good advertisements in both these ways—by *informing* others accurately about their faith and by *convincing* them of its supreme value. John's Gospel admits frankly to this double aim: 'These things have been written,' says John, 'in order that you may believe that Jesus is the Messiah, the Son of God, and that through your faith in him you may have life.'

Nevertheless, when a Christian sees an advertisement on a hoarding down the road, or between programmes on his TV, he has some critical questions to ask. Does it stretch the truth? Is it harmful? Is it wasteful? And does it promote wrong attitudes to life? As we take those points one by one, we shall discover various ways in which the advertisers' freedom should be limited in the interests of their customers.

Honesty

If honesty means telling everything, all advertising is dishonest. But that is being excessively harsh. You just cannot say everything there is to say about a car or a cake-mix in a thirty-second commercial. Inevitably, the advertiser deals in simplifications and selects his slogans to show off his product to its best advantage. The potential buyer knows that, and makes allowances for it.

It would be a very grey world, too, if humour were to be ruled out of advertising, in the name of honesty. As I write this chapter a series of television commercials is publicizing a beer which 'reaches parts other beers can't reach'. You see a tired policeman's toes begin to twitch when he has sunk a pint of this amazing product, and a Australian aborigine suddenly finds the strength to make his boomerangs come back. It's all unbelievable nonsense of course, but you have to chuckle at the ad-man's ingenuity—and the name of his product sticks in your mind.

Deliberate attempts to deceive the consumer come in a quite different, more serious moral category. The Bible never white-washes blatant dishonesty in doing business. 'All who do such things,' says the Old Testament law (with sharp salesmen who weight their scales in mind), 'all who act dishonestly, are an abomination to the Lord your God.' Twentieth-century methods of duping the customer are more sophisticated (as when they use a wide-angled camera lens to exaggerate the distance between rows of seats on a plane), but they stand condemned by the same biblical principle. Christians will therefore put all their weight behind bodies like the Independent Broadcasting Authority and the Advertising Standards Authority which exist to clip the wings of advertisers who cheat.

The truth is that very few advertisers are deliberately and consistently dishonest. But many of them regularly practise a more subtle kind of deception which is perfectly legal but a legitimate cause for concern to anyone with moral scruples. The dishonesty (if that is the right word) is not so much in the specific claims made about the product as in the fringe benefits implied by the way it is put across.

If you use a particular brand of perfume, for example, or smoke a special kind of pipe tobacco, you will have queues of admirers from the opposite sex—or so the commercials suggest. Buying a certain type of new car will automatically make you the envy of the neighbours and lift you several rungs up the status ladder. This kind of 'promise' can never be fulfilled, of course. Most customers make the necessary mental adjustments anyway when they see these advertisements. But the advertiser is not appealing to calculating minds. His message is aimed at the emotions. He is trying to tap deep reservoirs of human longing and aspiration, and some of his victims undoubtedly dream his dreams and take his suggestions at face value—however much it is against their better judgement to do so. When that happens, and disappointment follows, the ad-man must surely shoulder some of the blame.

Harm

Do advertisements actually harm people, by persuading them to buy things they would be better off without, or don't really want? This is a crucial area for debate, but before we explore it there is an important distinction to clarify.

We must distinguish carefully between the *product* that is advertised and the *method* used to publicize it. Some products are recognizably bad in themselves—a book advocating rape, for example, or a do-it-yourself guide to drug addiction. Other things, like cigarettes and alcoholic drink, would be regarded as bad by some people, particularly if taken in excess. It is obviously immoral to promote the sale of anything which is bad, or to encourage excessive consumption of something that is dangerous in large doses, even if the advertising techniques used are completely fair. Different people will have different black-lists, of course, but the basic principle remains. If the thing itself is bad, it has to be wrong to advertise it.

Moral problems multiply, however, when we consider

different ways of advertising perfectly innocent products. We have already turned the spotlight on a certain kind of advertisement which makes its appeal at a sub-rational level, playing on the customer's hopes and fears to make a quick sale. Taken to its extreme, that adds up to brain-washing. Promotional techniques which use powerful psychological devices to by-pass the mind (subliminal advertising) are outlawed in Britain and elsewhere, and Christians will always want to support this kind of legal restraint which defends the individual's right to be treated as a thinking person with a capacity for choice.

Here, though, our moral judgements have to be fine-tuned. We are all complex bundles of mind and emotions, and the advertiser is quite within his moral rights to appeal to us as we are. He may be wrong to persuade us to buy a drug by making us afraid of getting a disease we shall probably never catch, but he is hardly being immoral if he tries to sell us a life insurance policy by stressing *all* the wounds of bereavement—personal as well as financial.

Some people, of course, are far more at risk from frankly emotional appeals than others. Children are particularly vulnerable, and again Christians will want to give their full support to Codes of Advertising Practice like that of the British Independent Broadcasting Authority which aim to stop advertisers taking advantage of a child's natural credulity and sense of loyalty. It is a basic principle of biblical law that the weak should be protected from exploitation.

Waste

Perhaps the most powerful criticism of the advertising industry today is the charge that it is a parasite on the economy. It creates nothing of any value itself, while it adds to the cost of everything on which it feeds. That raises particularly big questions for Christians in the light of the Bible's teaching on stewardship. So why not scrap advertising altogether and

GUIDELINES FOR ADVERTISERS

● Harm
'Advertisements for the following must not be transmitted during children's programmes or in the advertisement breaks immediately before or after them—i.e. alcoholic drinks and liqueur chocolates, cigars, tobacco and matches . . . For reasons of dental hygiene advertisements shall not encourage persistent sweet eating throughout the day nor the eating of sweet, sticky foods at bed-time.'
IBA Code

'Jesus said to his disciples, "Things that make people fall into sin are bound to happen, but how terrible for the one who makes them happen! It would be better for him if a large millstone were tied round his neck and he were thrown into the sea than for him to cause one of these little ones to sin".'
The Bible—Luke 17:1-2

● Honesty
'The general principle which will govern all broadcast advertising is that it should be legal, decent, honest and truthful.'
The IBA Code of Advertising Standards and Practice

'Do not steal or cheat or lie.'
The Bible—Leviticus 19:11

● Waste
'No advertisement shall encourage, directly or indirectly indiscriminate, unnecessary or excessive use of products.'
IBA Code, on medicines

'When they were all full, Jesus said to his disciples, "Gather the pieces left over; let us not waste any".'
The Bible—John 6:12

● Greed
'Advertisements must not feature or foster immoderate drinking.'
IBA Code

'I have learnt to be satisfied with what I have.'
The Bible—Philippians 4:11

devote the proceeds to bringing down prices in the shops?

Ultimately, this is a challenge not just to advertising but to the competitive capitalist system which spawned it and which makes it necessary. Within that system, the advertiser can defend himself more than adequately. Good publicity, he would point out, leads to bigger **sales, which in turn result in** *lower* prices in the shops and higher employment in the factories. Moreover, there is obvious value in the fierce competition that advertising stimulates. It keeps profits in check, ensures that consumers always have a choice and provides manufacturers with incentives to make new and improved products. Even the Russians have had to introduce advertising to spur reluctant producers to greater efforts!

There is a less rosy side to the picture too. If a firm spends a million pounds advertising a washing powder, all its competitors have to mount similar campaigns to publicize virtually identical products,

just to stay in the race. One way or another the consumer has to foot the bill, and it is hard to pretend that no waste is involved, even if the proceeds do help to keep some people in paid work. Is this the unacceptable face of capitalism? Opinions will differ, and there is no space here to discuss them. But those who live happily under a competitive system should at least be aware of its weaknesses, and be prepared to check its more obvious failings.

Values

The IBA's Code of Advertising Standards and Practice demands that all advertising should be 'legal, decent, honest and truthful'. That is an admirable general principle, but in practice it leaves too many loop-holes to satisfy a Christian's conscience. Frequent appeals in advertisements to vanity, envy and self-gratification make Christians feel particularly uncomfortable. There is also something distinctly sub-Christian in the sense of restless discontent that some advertisers try to stimulate in order to sell their products. 'Consume more and be happier' is a slogan that is very hard to reconcile with Christ's warning, 'Guard yourselves from every kind of greed; because a person's true life is not made up of the things he owns.'

We must be careful not to make scapegoats out of the advertisers. The reason they appeal to our greed is because we are greedy people. They do not create the self-centred qualities which their publicity highlights. They simply mirror and focus what is already there. But in reflecting those more shady aspects of human nature they are in fact reinforcing the very things the Christian gospel seeks to change.

Here, probably, is the most important pointer we can find towards a Christian contribution to the world of advertising. Advertisers are particularly sensitive to public opinion. They must monitor it accurately in order to be effective. Criticism of particular kinds of publicity is therefore treated very seriously by the agencies, especially if it is sustained. But unless such criticism is merely negative and artificial, it must itself reflect genuine swings in public opinion. And the Christian gospel is in business to bring about exactly that kind of positive change in society. As one Christian advertising executive puts it, 'If Christians devoted more of their energies to awakening public opinion, this could achieve far more success than constantly complaining about the advertising profession itself.'

8 VIOLENCE

CAN WAR EVER BE JUSTIFIED?

Christian opinion on pacifism is split right down the middle. But everyone is agreed on one thing at least. War is an evil. Some television films glamorize fighting, but we only have to switch channels and watch the news to see how horrific modern warfare actually is in real life. Children screaming with napalm burns, men searching for their families in the burned-out ruins of their homes, and long lines of trudging refugees—they all remind us how stupid it is to dress war up in romantic disguise and idolize its heroes.

God hates war too. The Bible leaves us in no doubt about that. When the Messiah comes, Isaiah forecast, he will be called 'the Prince of Peace'. 'He will settle disputes among great nations. They will hammer their swords into ploughs and their spears into pruning-knives. Nations will never again go to war, never prepare for battle again.'

Nevertheless, we cannot just wish wars away. Jesus was a realist in this respect. He spoke well of a soldier, without so much as a hint that he should change his job. Quite often he used battle situations to illustrate his teaching, and he predicted tragic world-wide conflicts before his second coming when his rule of peace would at last be established. Indeed, the Bible goes much further than simply accepting the fact of war. The Old Testament in particular teaches that God uses warfare as one of his ways to right the world's wrongs. He is a 'God of battles', teaching his people to fight, and heading their army in combat.

All this leaves the Christian in a difficult position. Facing the horror of the mushroom cloud, as well as the deadly nature of conventional modern weapons, should he make a stand for God's ideals of peace and reconciliation by becoming a pacifist? Or should he reluctantly agree to fight, as the least evil course of action open to him when an international mugger threatens to go berserk? Is the right slogan 'Peace at any cost' or 'Justice at any price'?

Pacifism—yes?

The teaching and example of Jesus convince many Christians that they should be pacifists. After all, he told his disciples to *love* their enemies, and he stretched the commandment 'You shall not kill' (which, to be fair, was never meant to include killing in battle) to cover hatred in the mind and heart as well. A few minutes spent watching a session of bayonet practice is enough to make anyone realize what is involved—the only way a soldier can bring himself to plunge in the blade is to fortify himself with hate, even when the target is just a dummy. It is true that modern warfare makes killing less personal by doing most of it at long-range, but even if you do not actually hate the people at the receiving end of your missiles, it is very hard to love them while you press the firing button.

Jesus backed his teaching on non-violence by his example. He stopped Peter using his sword in the Garden of Gethsemane. And a few hours later he chose to suffer an unjust death rather than call on the overwhelming force which was there for him to use, had he wanted to stand up for his rights. 'Your life must be controlled by love, just as Christ loved us,' wrote Paul. Surely, argues the pacifist, following Christ's example bans Christians from ever fighting in a war. As the Anglican bishops resolved at three Lambeth Conferences spanning World War II, 'War as a method of settling international disputes is incompatible with the teaching and example of our Lord Jesus Christ.'

There are other, more practical arguments in favour of pacifism. For one thing, war is a terrible waste of resources. At a time when 40 per cent of the world's population is on the brink of starvation, over £100,000 million is spent annually on armaments. That has to be wrong. So, too, is the suggestion that war is justified by its results. Slogans from the first World War like 'the war to end all wars' sound very hollow now. And the outcome of World War II, which was fought to destroy German and Japanese imperialism, has been the re-arming of those same two nations to combat new threats to world peace. War breeds war, in what Archbishop Camara of Brazil has called 'a spiral of violence'. History shows that champions of passive resistance, such as Gandhi and Martin Luther King, have a far greater long-term influence for peace and change.

. . . or no?

Many Christians are among those who cannot accept pacifism. They see Jesus' teaching in an entirely different light. He certainly taught non-resistance in personal relation-ships, they agree, but international relationships are different altogether. It may be right to turn the other cheek when someone hits *me*, but that doesn't excuse me if I stand back with my arms folded when a violent man strikes *someone else*. A head of government must always be thinking of the 'someone elses'—not only the present and future citizens of his own country, but also the men and women of other nations who suffer aggression. As well as loving his enemy, he must love his enemy's victims. And that may cast him in a policeman's role, using force where necessary to restrain international bullies. How else could Churchill and Roosevelt have shown love for the Jews, who suffered such atrocities under Hitler? It is not for nothing that so many war memorials have Jesus' words inscribed over the names of their dead, 'The greatest love a person can have for his friends is to give his life for them.'

The hawk's strongest argument against the dove is an appeal to justice. A small nation may be 'pacified' by a more powerful aggressor, but the voice of oppression cries out for redress. An old lady will give up her handbag if her arm is twisted hard enough, but that doesn't mean passers-by can rest content when she stops struggling. The only thing muggers understand is forcible restraint, whether they operate solo in small towns or with armies on the international scene. It is a foolishly starry-eyed view of human nature to pretend that 'right will triumph in the end' if nothing is ever done to counter injustice.

Many of those who decide it is right to fight in a war respect conscientious objectors, but they have some hard questions to put to them. Is it right, they ask, to accept a community's privileges if you are not prepared to take your share in defending them? This puts the pacifist in a very different spot. He may prefer to surrender his privileges, but in the modern world that is often impossible. There are just not enough desert islands to go round. Even if he decides to pull his weight by taking a job on a farm instead of fighting, he still ends up supporting the war effort by paying his taxes and growing food to feed the servicemen.

Just war in the nuclear age

The theory of the 'just war' is a mid-way position between the extreme pacifist on the one hand and the extreme patriot ('my country right or wrong') on the other. Its roots go deep into pre-Christian history, but Augustine (AD 400) and Thomas Aquinas (AD 1250) adapted it to provide guidelines for puzzled Christians facing conscription in wartime. From one point of view, it lays down limits for participation in war. From the other, it supports selective conscientious objection.

The theory itself stands on four legs. First it lays down the rule that *a war must be declared by the properly constituted authority* if it is to be just. This bans impulsive reaction to international incidents and makes the declaration of hostilities a last resort, after diplomacy has failed at every level. Second, *war must have a just cause*. Apart from self-defence, this only justifies armed conflict if an aggressor refuses to restore what he has seized. Third, *war must have a just aim*. The aim must match the cause, so that all fighting stops as soon as the particular wrong that made war necessary has been put right. It also means that the ultimate goal is to restore good relations with the enemy, not to humiliate him. And finally, *war must be waged in a just way*. Traditionally this has been understood to put two limits on the way any war is waged: first by restricting the amount of force to the maximum needed for the war's limited objectives to be achieved; and second, by ensuring the safety of non-combatants and all those not directly involved in the war effort.

The word 'traditionally' gives the game away, of course! Modern weaponry makes a nonsense of the distinction between combatants and non-combatants. Even so-called 'conventional' means of waging war today are so devastating as to make such discrimination virtually impossible. The fighting in Vietnam illustrated that in a particularly vivid, horrifying way. And when the terrors of thermo-nuclear conflict are brought into the reckoning, it seems impossible ever to meet this fourth condition of a just war. Once the warheads are armed and the missiles are launched, farmers and babies will die as surely as soldiers and munition-workers. There can be no discrimination in the slaughter. Nor can there be any pretence that the force used is limited to the war's immediate objective. Radioactivity con-taminates neutrals, threatens the lives of unborn generations (should there be any) and destroys nature.

Does this mean the old 'just war' theory should be pensioned off—or that modern Christians should be nuclear pacifists? Again, opinions differ. The Bible's teaching offers guidelines, not directives. The guiding principles all Christians share are those of *love* and *justice*. When the two point in the same direction, finding the right way is no problem. But in this broken world their signals often conflict. It is particularly hard to think of any situation where pressing the nuclear

WHERE DO WARS COME FROM?

'What causes wars, and what causes fightings among you? Is it not your passions that are at war in your members? You desire and do not have; so you kill. And you covet and cannot obtain; so you fight and wage war.'
The Bible—James 4:1, 2

'If sunbeams were weapons of war, we would have had solar energy centuries ago.'
Sir George Porter, Nobel Laureate in Chemistry

THE LIMITS OF NATIONALISM

'When a State has the chance to improve its position because of the weakness of a neighbour, do you think it will stop at any squeamish consideration of keeping a promise? It is a statesman's duty to take advantage of such a situation for the good of his country.'
Hermann Goering

'"The national interest" can too easily deteriorate from a needed and legitimate concern for the common good to a mask for unadulterated selfishness at whatever cost to others.'
Arthur Holmes

LOVE FOR ENEMIES—AND OTHERS

'The New Testament says, "If thine enemy hunger, feed him"; modern war says, "If thine enemy hunger, tighten the blockade".'
P. Hartill

'It is part of the tragedy of living that sometimes the claims of love from different people are incompatible, and one has to be chosen before another. The command that we should love our enemies does not mean that we should love our enemies alone ... It is a caricature of Christian love to love your enemy to the detriment of your friends.'
T. E. Jessop

PACIFISM—THE CHRISTIAN ANSWER?

'For we no longer take sword against a nation nor do we learn any more to make war, having become sons of peace for the sake of Jesus who is our leader.'
Origen, AD 185-254

'It is right to occupy oneself with the sword when the Lord proclaims that he who uses the sword shall perish by the sword? How shall Christians wage war, nay, how shall he even be a soldier in peace time, without the sword which the Lord has taken away?'
Tertullian, AD 160-230

'It is lawful for Christian men, at the commandment of the Magistrate to wear weapons, and serve in the wars.'
Article 37 of the Church of England

'Far better some years of "total war" with its misery and waste and increasing bitterness of spirit, than the riveting of that diabolical (Nazi) system upon more and more people.'
William Temple

'If the Christian accepts the privileges of community life, he must not try to escape its responsibilities.

Even if he tries, he cannot altogether do so ... The tax-payer who pays for the atomic bomb is as responsible for its use as the airman who drops it.'
William Lillie

NUCLEAR WAR—DIFFERENT IN KIND OR DEGREE?

'Before the thermo-nuclear bomb, man had to live with the idea of his death as an individual; from now onwards, mankind has to live with the idea of its death as a species.'
Arthur Koestler

'In this age which boasts of its atomic power, it no longer makes sense to maintain that war is a fit instrument with which to repair the violation of justice.'
Pope John XXIII

'The clean prophetic stance of nuclear pacifism which may be admirable in an individual may be a social impossibility.'
John Mahoney

'The alternatives presented by the pacifists and nuclear disarmers are not in the end a higher view of human life but the lower view—for, if faced with the issue to live without any of the things that give life value and make it worthwhile or to die to preserve those things, it is better to die.'
T. E. Jessop

---

button could ever be called loving, even if it could be defended as just. In such dilemmas there are only second-best options available. The choice is between the frying-pan and the fire. It will lead some Christians to take up arms, reluctantly, in a conventional war. It will deter most from participating

A nuclear warhead is tested in the Australian desert. The classic theory of the 'just war' taught that war must be waged at a level appropriate to its aims. But can such a concept mean anything in a generation where the nuclear firepower exists to kill the world population several times over?

actively in a nuclear conflict.

There is another special dimension, however, to the Bible's teaching on war and peace. According to the New Testament, human conflict is only a projection of the greater cosmic war between the forces of good and the forces of evil. At the supernatural level, where it matters most, the result has already been settled and decided. 'On the cross,' wrote Paul, 'Christ stripped the spiritual rulers and authorities of their power.' This is the bright ray of hope the Christian faith sees in the nuclear darkness. Whatever God allows to happen in

the immediate future, the Christian knows that the end of world history will reveal the Prince of Peace reigning in total triumph.

8 VIOLENCE

SHOULD PEOPLE BE PUNISHED?

It hardly seems right to call punishment 'violence'. And yet, however you look at it, punishing people hurts them. It does so most obviously when a murderer is executed. But even discipline in the home involves violence of a kind. Father may say, 'This hurts me more than it hurts you,' but a smack on the bottom would be useless unless it caused pain! The hurt need not be physical. It may take the form of a fine or a prison sentence. But whether the result is lost freedom or lost money, some violence has been done to the person who suffers the punishment.

The big question that faces the Christian is whether it is ever right to hurt others. Jesus taught non-violence. He said, 'If anyone slaps you on the right cheek, let him slap your left cheek too.' Does that rule out any means of restraining or deterring those who do wrong?

There are three main ways of looking at punishment. The scene changes as the focus shifts from the crime to the criminal to the community. As we explore these three approaches, we shall try to see how Christian teaching relates to each.

The crime

If you focus on the crime, your main aim in punishing the offender will be to see that he suffers justly for what he has done. The penalty will be really harsh if the crime is vicious, and more lenient if it is trivial. In other words, the guiding principle will always be 'Let the punishment fit the crime.'

There is plenty to be said in favour of this approach. For one thing, it treats crime consistently. Offenders themselves recognize the fairness of 'getting your deserts'. As

C. S. Lewis put it, 'Punishment is treating a person as a human being—giving him what he knows he deserves.' There is a certain dignity in being brought face to face with your responsibilities and paying the right price for what you have done.

Sometimes the objection is raised that this attitude to punishment is really nothing more than the urge to hit back, dressed up in the robes of justice to make it look respectable. As we have seen, Jesus forbade all revenge. But this is not really a fair criticism. Jesus was talking about personal retaliation. A judge who passes sentence is not being vengeful. He is simply fixing the just penalty for an offence committed against someone else—which is why the person wronged is never allowed to inflict the punishment.

The principle of retribution is deeply embedded in the Bible. Indeed, the Old Testament's penal system was built on it. 'If anyone injures another person,' says the law of Leviticus, 'whatever he has done shall be done to him.' The New Testament strikes the same note in describing the judgement of God. When we appear before Christ, writes Paul, 'each one will receive what he deserves'.

Nevertheless, there are severe drawbacks in a blinkered view of punishment which refuses to look any further than the crime. For one thing, it appears *unconstructive*—dealing with one injury only by adding another. More seriously, it may turn out to be *unfair*, by ignoring extenuating circumstances and diminished responsibility. If all parking offences must be punished in the same way, it becomes impossible to distinguish between the couldn't-care-less social menace who leaves his car in a No Waiting zone to save a walk to the cinema and the doctor who parks there because it is the nearest point to the scene of an accident. If there is the same fixed penalty for everyone caught stealing from shops, the greedy sneak-thief and the kleptomaniac who needs medical help have to be treated in an identical way. And that is less than just.

It is this kind of consideration that sets the scene for the next approach:

The criminal

Many today would go along with Bernard Shaw when he wrote, 'To punish is to injure; to reform is to heal. You cannot mend a person by damaging him.' The focus of punishment, they would say, must be on the offender, not the offence. Therefore the right question to ask is not 'What penalty does this crime deserve?' but 'How can this wrong-doer best be helped?'

This approach makes the law far less of a blunt instrument. It allows a court to treat six shop-lifters in six different ways, tailoring the punishment to fit each thief. It also gives the sentencing judge or magistrate scope to be constructive. He can fix penalties with a view to reforming offenders, and so do his best to bring some good out of bad situations.

Obviously, the stress this view of punishment lays on the offender as a person finds strong echoes in Jesus' teaching. Think of the way he dealt with the woman caught in the act of adultery, and the parable of the prodigal son (the young man who forfeited all his rights by the way he behaved, but who was rehabilitated by his father instead of being forced to pay the just penalty).

But despite its attractions there are as many risks in this second approach as there were in the first. It may, for example, leave an impression of *injustice*, which alienates both wrong-doers and victims. If one man suffers a heavier penalty than another for exactly the same offence, he naturally resents the discrimination. And a person who has been wronged will feel unfairly treated, too, if the offender gets off particularly lightly. A light sentence may also *detract from the seriousness of the crime*. It might make good sense to give a child murderer probation instead of a prison sentence as the best means of rehabilitating him, but the impression left in the minds of those who read the newspaper reports is that playing fast and loose with

THE DIMENSIONS OF PUNISHMENT

● Retribution

'To deny the retributive element in punishment is to deny any meaning to the words merit, justice and—I think—forgiveness.'
Carritt

'The concept of desert is the only connecting link between punishment and justice.'
C. S. Lewis

'A person will reap exactly what he sows.'
The Bible—Galatians 6:7

● Reform

'If offenders are to respect the law, their own basic rights must not be brushed aside. The appalling physical conditions and lack of constructive activity which persist in many prisons should not be tolerated in a civilized society.'
The Howard League for Penal Reform

'The teachers of the Law and the Pharisees brought in a woman who had been caught committing adultery . . . "Teacher," they said to Jesus, "in our Law Moses commanded that such a woman must be stoned to death. Now, what do you say?" . . . He said to them, "Whichever one of you has committed no sin may throw the first stone at her." . . . He said to her, "Where are they? Is there no one left to condemn you?" "No one, sir," she answered. "Well, then," Jesus said, "I do not condemn you either. Go, but do not sin again".'
The Bible—John 8:3–11

● Deterrence

'The state and its system of criminal justice can do no more than adopt such measures to defend the community against criminals as are reasonable in themselves and proportionate to the danger threatened to society.'
Enrico Ferri

'Capital punishment builds up in the community, over a long period of time, a deep feeling of peculiar abhorrence for the crime of murder.'
Royal Commission on Capital Punishment

'Then the men of the city are to stone him to death, and so you will get rid of this evil. Everyone in Israel will hear what has happened and be afraid.'
The Bible—Deuteronomy 21:21

● Reparation

'If you think—as I do—that criminals ought to make some genuine financial restitution to the victims of their crimes, do stop to reflect that if you insist that they mustn't be paid more than a few shillings a week, there is something wrong with your logic.'
Bernard Levin

'If a man steals a cow or a sheep and kills it or sells it, he must pay five cows for one cow and four sheep for one sheep. He must pay for what he stole.'
The Bible—Exodus 22:1, 2

death for those offenders whose continued presence spelled great danger for the community. But, as with the two other approaches, there are serious problems if deterrence is made the *only* consideration. In particular, it is all too easy, in the attempt to put society's interests first, to trample on the rights of the individual. A heavy deterrent sentence could be passed on a shop-lifter, for example, to persuade others not to imitate him, but the penalty might be out of all proportion to the particular crime he had committed. Pushed to its extreme, this attitude to punishment would even justify the execution of an innocent person. As Caiaphas put it, with his eye on Jesus, 'It may be expedient for one man to die for the people.'

By now it will be obvious that the Bible encourages us to strike a balance between these three views of punishment, not to choose between them. That does not make for easy decisions. It also explains why Christians sometimes differ in their opinions on specific issues. To complete this chapter, we will take a quick look at two such themes, imprisonment and capital punishment, not in any hope of resolving them, but to clarify the arguments most often used on one side or the other.

Imprisonment

As an appropriate punishment for *crime*, a prison sentence is of dubious value. It prevents the offender making any restitution to the person he has harmed, and it effectively removes him from the effects of the trouble he has caused. Naturally, his sense of personal responsibility for what he has done is also dimmed. In this respect the Old Testament's penal system is an improvement on ours, in that it makes punishment far less anonymous. A mugger, for example, had to pay his victim's medical expenses in Old Testament times, as well as compensating him for working time lost as a result of his injuries.

The prison system fares little better when the spotlight moves

children's lives cannot be quite so serious a crime as they once thought. And that may put even more children at risk.

The community

As the focus shifts to public opinion and public safety, deterrence becomes the main consideration. What matters most, people say, is that society is protected from disruptive elements—and the best way of achieving that goal is by deterring those who would otherwise lead anti-social lives. As we shall see, this is the atmosphere in which capital

punishment is debated today. So the most pressing question becomes not 'Do murderers deserve to die?' or even 'How best can we reform murderers?' but 'How can we stop the murder rate increasing?'

Once more, there are parts of the Bible which clearly reflect this point of view. Over and over again, the Old Testament law justifies severe penalties for serious offences with the refrain, 'In this way you shall put away this evil from among you.' Because there were no maximum security cell blocks in ancient Israel, that usually meant from the crime to the *criminal*. When inmates are crowded three to a small, stinking cell and prevented from working for a living wage, the atmosphere is hardly conducive to rehabilitation. Nor does a system of punishment which collects together people with similar weaknesses make their reform any more likely. Added to that, prison gets people used to life in an institution, making it even harder for prisoners to fit into the society they have wronged once they get out. All this makes the remedial value of a spell in the cells very doubtful indeed.

The strongest argument in favour of imprisonment is that, by removing the criminal from the public scene, it gives the *community* a breathing-space. The long-term prospects, however, are not nearly so rosy from society's point of view. There is little evidence to suggest that imprisonment is an effective deterrent. Prison sentences have doubled and trebled, but so has the crime rate. Undoubtedly there are some violent criminals who cannot be left free. Christians will not, therefore, want to campaign for the instant abolition of all prisons. But on Christian grounds there are enough drawbacks in the present system to make the search for alternatives an essential task.

Capital punishment

In contrast to the debate about imprisonment, the strongest possible argument in favour of capital punishment for murder comes when you consider *the crime*. Death is an obviously appropriate penalty for cold-blooded, criminal killing. The Bible makes the same point, and supports it by appealing to the principle of the sanctity of human life. 'Any man who murders shall be killed,' says the Old Testament, 'for to kill a man is to kill one made in God's image.'

Considering the *criminal*, on the other hand, leads to exactly the opposite conclusion. The death penalty allows for last-minute repentance but for little else in the way or reform or reparation. And if it is applied automatically, it leaves no room for mitigating circum-stances or diminished responsibility.

Some would argue that any murderer must be mentally unbalanced at the time he commits the crime.

The case for the *community* can be pressed either way. It is by no means clear how far the prospect of facing an executioner would deter the average murderer. Generally speaking, most policemen are sure that it would and most psychologists are equally certain that it wouldn't. As so often, the statistics can be made to support either point of view. The educational value of the death penalty is hotly debated too. Some claim that capital punishment reinforces society's abhorrence of murder, but few would want to see a repeat of the first 'educational' railway excursion in Britain—which took trippers to see a public execution in Somerset.

Taking the three approaches together, there is perhaps room here for a proper compromise. However murder is punished, the penalty must reflect the enormity of the offence. But this must be balanced by concern for the offender (because the Christian believes no one is past hope), and by the need for an effective social deterrent. If the death penalty is thought to be the answer, it means there must be generous allowance for reprieve to satisfy those concerns which centre on the criminal. If it isn't, the chosen alternative must be severe enough to be appropriate to the crime and satisfactory for the community.

8 VIOLENCE

HOW FAR SHOULD CIVIL PROTEST GO?

'Keep religion out of politics.' You often hear that said, both by politicians (especially when church leaders challenge them) and by ordinary people. Religion, as many see it, is about other-worldly things only. Surely Jesus said as much when he told Pontius Pilate, Rome's political chief in Judea, 'My kingdom does not belong to this world.' His last command to his disciples was not 'Go and put society to rights', but 'Go and preach the gospel'. Religious people should therefore leave social issues to the politicians (it is said) and concentrate on living the life of the spirit.

Down the ages, some Christians have tried to do exactly that. As early as AD 423 a man called Simeon built himself a pillar and sat on top of it for thirty-seven years, so he could say his prayers in peace without being disturbed by the rush and bustle of life below. Later, in medieval times, some monks bricked themselves up in their cells. A visitor asked one man who had been in that state for twenty-five years whether he was still alive. 'I believe I am dead to the world,' came the triumphant reply. For him, religion meant living as though the outside world did not exist.

All this, however, is a travesty of the Bible's teaching. The Old Testament taught that the whole of life should be lived in a God-centred way. It assumed that God's will applied as much to the believer's economic and political life (when he lent money, got the harvest in or administered justice) as it did to his private, spiritual life. The Ten Commandments, the pivot on which the Old Testament law turned, set out obligations to society alongside obligations to

THE BIBLE ON ATTITUDES TO CIVIL AUTHORITY

● Co-operation

Jesus said, "Well, then, pay the Emperor what belongs to the Emperor, and pay God what belongs to God".
Mark 12:17

'Everyone must obey the state authorities, because no authority exists without God's permission, and the existing authorities have been put there by God. Whoever opposes the existing authority opposes what God has ordered; and anyone who does so will bring judgement on himself. For rulers are not to be feared by those who do good, but by those who do evil . . . For this reason you must obey the authorities—not just because of God's punishment, but also as a matter of conscience.'
Romans 13:1-3, 5

'Pay taxes, because the authorities are working for God when they fulfil their duties. Pay, then, what you owe them; pay them your personal and property taxes, and show respect and honour for them all.'
Romans 13:6, 7

'First of all, then, I urge that petitions, prayers, requests, and thanksgivings be offered to God for all people; for kings and all others who are in authority, that we may live a quiet and peaceful life with all reverence towards God and with proper conduct.'
1 Timothy 2:1, 2

● Resistance

'When Ahab saw Elijah, he said, "Have you caught up with me, my enemy?" "Yes, I have," Elijah answered. "You have devoted yourself completely to doing what is wrong in the Lord's sight. So the Lord says to you, 'I will bring disaster on you . . .!'".'
1 Kings 21:20-21

'The king said to them, "Shadrach, Meshach, and Abednego, is it true that you refuse to worship my God and to bow down to the gold statue I have set up?" . . . Shadrach, Meshach, and Abednego answered, "Your Majesty, we will not try to defend ourselves. If the God whom we serve is able to save us from the blazing furnace and from your power, then he will. But even if he doesn't, Your Majesty may be sure that we will not worship your god,

and we will not bow down to the gold statue that you have set up".'
Daniel 3:14, 16-18

'Herod himself had ordered John's arrest, and he had him chained and put in prison. Herod did this because of Herodias, whom he had married, even though she was the wife of his brother Philip. John the Baptist kept telling Herod, "It isn't right for you to be married to your brother's wife!"'
Mark 6:17, 18

'The next morning the Roman authorities sent police officers with the order, "Let those men go." So the jailer told Paul, "The officials have sent an order for you and Silas to be released. You may leave, then, and go in peace." But Paul said to the police officers, "We were not found guilty of any crime, yet they whipped us in public— and we are Roman citizens! Then they threw us in prison. And now they want to send us away secretly. Not likely! The Roman officials themselves must come and let us out".'
Acts 16:35-37

CHRISTIANS AND REVOLUTION

'The Church condemns violence, but it condemns indifference more harshly. Violence can be the expression of love, indifference never.'
Graham Greene

'Nor could I, for one, *absolutely* exclude the permissibility, in extreme circumstances, of what may be termed tyrannicide: for I could not, for example, condemn Bonhoeffer, formerly a convinced pacifist, for his conviction that Hitler was so evil, and so deeply stained with innocent blood, that he had no option but to participate in a plot to destroy him.'
Sir Norman Anderson

'It is not possible to issue a blanket condemnation of all who under any circumstances resort to violence. Where protests against injustice have been stilled by promises of redress which remain unfulfilled, it is governments who bear the heaviest responsibility for violence which may thus break out.'
The Roman Catholic Bishops of England and Wales

'Christians who side with the oppressed and justify violence on their behalf cannot, for all their

goodwill and seeming charity, be counted among the meek, nor among the merciful, nor among the peacemakers, nor yet among those who hunger and thirst for justice . . . Once you start violence, you cannot get away from it . . . It is impossible to distinguish between justified and unjustified violence, between violence that liberates and violence that enslaves.'
Jacques Ellul

'The problem with revolutions from the Christian vantage-point is not that they are too radical but that they are not radical enough. They are an attempt to eradicate violent societies by violent means. They are based on over-optimistic estimates of human goodness and perfectibility . . . The problem with violent revolutions is not that they change too much, but that they change too little. Socialist Utopias have not changed the nature of man. Czech and Soviet workers are still as selfishly concerned about their pay-cheques as are their unregenerate counterparts in the West.'
Alan Kreider

'We shall match your capacity to inflict suffering by our capacity to endure suffering. We shall meet your physical force with soul force. Do to us what you will and we shall continue to love you. One day we shall win freedom, but not only for ourselves. We shall so appeal to your heart and conscience that we shall win you in the process, and our victory will be a double victory.'
Martin Luther King

'The Christian approach to government differs from the anarchical concept in several ways. It gladly *obeys* where government observes its proper limits, *protests* where it exceeds those limits, and *actively resists* where a totalitarian demand requires disobedience to the revealed will of God.'
Carl Henry

God. And when Jesus summed them all up in his two famous love commands, he packed 'love your neighbour' with such social meaning that the religious and political leaders of his day quickly branded him a dangerous revolutionary.

Social obligations

Political life in Bible times was very different to life in a modern democracy, but the New Testament sets out four Christian social duties which are as relevant now as they were then. First, there is the very practical obligation to *pay taxes*. When Jesus was asked a trick question about paying tax to the hated Roman authorities, the word he used for '*pay* the Emperor' meant '*pay back* a debt'. The apostle Paul uses the same word to reinforce Jesus' teaching—and by his time the Emperor had turned persecutor. Some of the revenue the first Christians paid to the tax-man went, no doubt, towards subsidizing their own imprisonment and execution. But the New Testament offers no excuses to Christians who decide to withhold their taxes as a protest against the way the money is spent. Failure to pay up is not a withdrawal of good-will, but a refusal to repay the debt every citizen owes to society for the services and amenities he cannot help using.

Paul immediately adds that Christians are also obliged to *respect those in civil authority*. A tax-collector in New Testament times was a social outcast once he left his office—and for very good reasons. It would have been far easier to pay him your money than give him your respect. His counterparts in the twentieth century may not work in tax offices, but most of us know politicians and others who use their authority in such petty ways that they deserve no respect at all. The New Testament distinguishes sharply between the office-holder and his role. A man may abuse his position, but if the structures of government are going to hold together, his office must never become an object of scorn.

Respect for civil authority also has a bearing on the Christian's third duty, which is to *pray for national leaders*. The main object of such prayer, writes Paul, is 'that we may live a quiet and peaceful life'. By that he meant security to move around freely, not a life of peace and quiet on a luxury yacht. As we shall see, the Bible treats the maintenance of law and order as a top responsibility for any government. The regime under which Paul lived was certainly not above criticism, but quite often he had reason to be extremely grateful for the quick, effective intervention of civil and military officials when his life was in danger. The implication is that Christians may only raise their arms in protest against government policy when they have first lowered their voices in prayer.

The fourth Christian duty is the most obvious one of all—the obligation to *aid society's casualties*. Jesus made this point unforgettably in his story of the Good Samaritan, the man who overcame barriers of racial prejudice and personal inconvenience to look after the mugger's unknown victim in the gutter. Christians are not the only people, of course, to spend time and effort on shut-ins and drop-outs, but this kind of social ambulance work will always be a top priority for those who want to express the kind of neighbour-love that Jesus taught.

Political protest

Here, however, we come face to face with the biggest political question Christians meet today. Is it adequate simply to treat society's *casualties*, without doing something about the root-cause of their suffering in society's *structures*? Is it enough, for example, to show love to victimized immigrants, if we do nothing to challenge the political structures that encourage racial discrimination? Should Christians rest content with paying their taxes, respecting authority, praying for their national leaders and doing social first-aid—or should they also recognize other, more pressing obligations including the duty to challenge social injustice wherever

they see it? And if they have that kind of duty, what can be done about it?

There are several things that can be done short of violence. One obvious means is *vocal protest*. We hear a great deal today about the 'silent majority'. If all those who felt strongly about injustice dared to open their mouths and say so, the chances of change would be very much greater. Certainly, speaking your mind is far safer in a modern democracy than it was under the totalitarian regimes of New Testament times.

A second, but more risky, form of protest is *civil disobedience*. On his way to execution, Sir Thomas More said, 'I am the king's good servant, but God's first.' He was echoing Jesus' words, 'Pay the Emperor what belongs to the Emperor, and pay God what belongs to God.' If the voice of human authority commands something that is clearly against God's will, the right Christian reaction is to disobey—and then face the consequences.

Violence

But suppose protest falls on deaf ears and civil disobedience ends in cruel martyrdom—without changing anything. Can it be morally right in cases like that to go one step further and resort to violence in the fight against injustice? Are there situations so intolerable and regimes so oppressive that Christians are under a moral obligation to join those who use force to resist them? Was Jefferson right when he said, 'Rebellion against tyrants is obedience to God'?

We are certainly familiar with the idea that only violence gets things done. Bombs in railway stations, hijackers in planes and hostages in embassies all grab the headlines regularly. Pressure-groups of all political and religious shades, from Palestinian Muslims to Irish Protestants and Catholics, use the weapons of terrorism to fight for justice as they see it.

Some Christians would defend the use of force as a last resort. Not surprisingly, most of those who argue this way come from parts of the world where oppression is a first-hand experience. The German theologian Bonhoeffer's part in the plot to kill Hitler is a famous example of that kind of thing from the history books, while in our own day Christians fight alongside Marxists in South America to topple unjust regimes, and freedom-fighters in South Africa get financial aid from the World Council of Churches to resist apartheid. Their case is simply that it is sometimes less evil to overthrow a government by force than to allow its oppression to continue. If all non-violent means have failed; if the suffering of armed rebellion is likely to be less severe than the injustice that provoked it; and if there is a strong probability that a revolution will establish a better regime than the old one—then (the argument goes) violence is justified. After all, didn't Jesus say it was part of his mission to 'set free the oppressed'? And while he was still in her womb, didn't Mary sing about the God who 'has brought down mighty kings from their thrones, and lifted up the lowly'? Surely, therefore, modern revolutionaries are simply carrying on God's work.

The fact remains, though, that Jesus did not act the part of a revolutionary. He rejected the role of political leader, 'marched' on his capital city peacefully mounted on a donkey, and chose to suffer death rather than fight for justice. And his first disciples followed his non-violent example. Though they quickly became known as 'those who have turned the world upside down' and riots often followed their preaching, they never deliberately incited violence.

It is sometimes suggested that New Testament Christians did not resort to force because they were powerless to do so. Rebellion would have been suicide because they had no political or military muscle. And Jesus did not challenge political structures by violence because that was not his personal destiny. His whole reason for coming into the world was to die on the cross, not to lead a revolution.

That argument has a hollow ring about it. Political revolutionaries did not stand much chance in Jesus' day, but there were plenty of them around, and from time to time they scored local successes as they harried the Romans. Jesus was, in fact, born into a political atmosphere as highly charged as in any South American republic. His occupied nation was on tip-toe, waiting for its militant Messiah. At least one—and possibly as many as five—of his closest followers were freedom-fighters, so he must have been constantly bombarded with revolutionary propaganda. The fact that he resisted these pressures himself, and *taught his disciples to do the same*, points to factors that go much deeper than his own personal vocation and a particular set of historical circumstances.

If we ask what those factors were, the Bible suggests two. First, there is the priority of *law and order*. 'God does not want us to be in disorder,' wrote Paul. His mind was on disruption in church life, but he was pointing to something vital in God's will for everyone and everything. The Ruler of the universe detests anarchy in any shape or form. As far as civil authorities are concerned, Paul puts this truth across in a way that would make any terrorist's hair curl. 'There is no government anywhere,' he says, 'that God has not placed in power.' He was not pretending, of course, that all heads of government are saints. A shining halo would certainly not have suited the Roman Emperor Nero. But he was stating—very firmly—that God wants people to be governed in an orderly way, and that he makes his own plans to that effect. The trouble with revolution, however just its cause, is that it threatens order. It is far easier to scrawl graffiti on a wall, plant bombs in supermarkets and shoot policemen than it is to work constructively for social improvement. Would-be revolutionaries should at least recognize that they are planning to blast apart the seams that hold society's fabric in place.

The second major reason for the New Testament's kid-gloved attitude to social structures is *the nature of Christian revolution*. It is really a matter of priorities. When Jesus told Pontius Pilate 'My kingdom does not belong to this world', he meant that the kind of change he wanted was far more radical than political reform could ever hope to achieve. He exploded the myth that social changes can alter people. He worked the other way round. The kind of revolution he sparked went deep to the heart of human nature, changing natural self-centredness to supernatural love as it worked itself out in social relationships. In these terms, the trouble with a revolution is that it changes too little, not too much. It smashes the frame while doing nothing to alter the picture. Jesus' aim was to revolutionize society by changing people.

To sum up, then, Christian teaching encourages full involvement in social affairs, not detachment from them. Positively, Christians have a clear duty to support those in authority with their money, their respect, their prayers and their caring energy. Faced by injustice, they have an equally clear duty to protest and (where necessary) to disobey. But violent revolution, because it disrupts order and fails to achieve the basic changes Jesus put first, is a course that few Christians would think it right to follow.

9 DOES GOD EXIST?

HOW CHRISTIANS THINK OF GOD

Christians, Jews and Muslims all believe that there is one supreme God who not only created the universe but who also cares for people. They describe what God is like in various ways. Islam, for example, has ninety-nine names for God, describing him by what he does, e.g. the Provider, the Decider, the Preserver, the Depriver. But the Bible's Old Testament uses vivid picture-language to describe him. God is:

'The high and lofty One'
'The holy One of Israel'
'The Rock'
'The Fortress'
'The Shepherd of Israel'
'The King'
'The Bridegroom'
'The Friend'
'The Father'

The picture of God as a rock suggests dependability. To speak of him as 'King' highlights the fact that he rules, and also that he is to be obeyed.

In the Christian New Testament the emphasis is on the picture of God as 'Father'. A good Jewish father ruled, provided and cared for his family. So this image shows us God's love, as well as his control. He offers a family relationship to those who trust him. Jesus himself loved to use the 'Father' picture of God. He describes himself as the unique and only Son of God the Father. The apostle Paul describes Christians as 'adopted children of God' brought into his family. He even encouraged us to call God 'Abba', the most intimate Jewish family father-word—virtually 'Dad'.

The Bible also gives us statements about God:

There are many passages in the Bible about the character of God. Here are some of them:

● **God is one:**
'Hear, O Israel: The Lord our God, the Lord is one. Love the Lord your God with all your heart and with all your soul and with all your strength.'
Deuteronomy 6:4, 5—the Jewish Shema

● **God is Creator:**
'In the beginning God created the heavens and the earth.'
Genesis 1:1

● **God is self-existent and changeless:**
'I am the Lord, and I do not change.'
Malachi 3:6—in the Old Testament, where our English Bibles have 'the Lord', the Hebrew is 'Yahweh' (Jehovah), which means 'the self-existent one'.

● **God is infinite:**
'Do you not know?
   Have you not heard?
Has it not been told you from the beginning?
Have you not understood since the earth was founded?
The Lord sits enthroned above the circle of the earth,
   and its people are like grasshoppers.

'God is wise'
'God is light'
'God is almighty'
'God is love'
These are general truths against which we can understand the picture-language.

All these metaphors and pictures combine to give us a very good idea of the richness of God's character and his relationship with his people. But they are not precise enough to provide clear answers to the questions 'Who is God?' and 'What is God like?' Because of this, there is another method of describing God, used by Christian thinkers, which suits people who want carefully prepared answers. They have tried to define in rational and philosophical terms the major principles and ideas conveyed by all the varied images and general statements found in the Bible.

We can summarize their conclusions in the following way.

He stretches out the heavens like a canopy,
   and spreads them out like a tent to live in.'
Isaiah 40:21, 22

● **God is eternal:**
'Before the mountains were born
   or you brought forth the earth and the world,
   from everlasting to everlasting you are God.'
Psalm 90:2

● **God is spirit:**
'God is spirit, and his worshippers must worship in spirit and in truth.'
John 4:24

● **God is perfect:**
'God is the Rock, his works are perfect,
   and all his ways are just.
A faithful God who does no wrong,
   upright and just is he.'
Deuteronomy 32:4

● **God relates to us personally:**
'Jesus said, "If anyone loves me, he will obey my teaching. My Father will love him, and we will come to him and make our home with him".'
John 14:23

First of all, by way of definition, Christians believe in one God, who is the Creator of the universe. He is self-existent, infinite, eternal, without body or shape, changeless, perfect, personal:

● **God is one** Some, such as Hindus, believe in many gods. Christians claim that there is only one God. This is 'monotheism'. The commitment to one God and the rejection of the non-gods of pagan religion was a distinguishing mark of the faith of ancient Israel. This same belief in one God is also basic for Christians. Their doctrine of the Trinity (see below) is wholly based on the idea of the unity of God.

● **God is the Creator** He made the universe, and he continues to sustain it. No form of life or being exists apart from his creative act. When God made it he placed within it what we call the laws of nature.

The majesty of creation moves many people to think about the Creator. But such feelings are usually rather vague. Can we say anything precise about what God is like?

He set the patterns, for example, which make it possible for us to say that the winter will follow the autumn.

● **God is self-existent** We owe our existence to our fathers and mothers. My typewriter exists because it was made in a factory. God is entirely different. Nothing, no one, is responsible for his existence. He is wholly and entirely self-sufficient.

● **God is infinite** There is no 'end' to God. He has none of the limitations which we have because we live in time and space.

● **God is eternal** God exists in a timeless present, not limited by past or future. We cannot escape from time. I cannot stop the minutes ticking by as I write these lines. But God made time when he made the universe and so he cannot be subject to it.

● **God is without body or shape** If God is 'infinite' and 'eternal', he must be non-spatial and thus bodiless. He is pure Spirit.

● **God is changeless** Since God is eternal he cannot change. To change is only possible within time. He does not grow up and grow old as we do. The fact of God's changelessness does not conflict with the Christian idea of praying for people and things. The purpose of prayer for others is not to change God or his will but to ask for what pleases him and is in harmony with his will.

● **God is perfect** The idea of perfection flows from the previous ideas. It also expresses the idea that he is 'holy': completely separate from evil. So God is perfectly holy, loving, righteous, just, wise. His knowledge and power are complete.

● **God is personal** As our Creator, God has made us in such a way that we can have a personal relationship with him. This is why we call him by such names as 'King', 'Father' and 'Shepherd'.

God always remains higher than our highest thoughts, greater than our most enlightened statements. Our words and phrases can only be signposts pointing to the amazing and wonderful reality which is God. But signposts must be accurate. Christians hold that this view of God is reliable. For it is based ultimately on Jesus himself.

9 DOES GOD EXIST?

SCIENCE AND GOD

The importance and prestige of science in our society is a fact of life. In harness with technology, science 'rules' modern society and makes us ever more dependent upon its advance. Each of the disciplines— physics, chemistry, biology, astronomy and so on—has made tremendous contributions not only to our knowledge of the world but also to our comfort and pleasure. Think of all that is involved in modern medicine and hospitals, modern rockets, planes and computers, and the TV and transistor radio in the home.

But it is fatally easy to overvalue the importance of science and to exaggerate its place in human experience. Science is of immense value in its proper field—it can explain many things and provide a means of dealing with a great range of technical problems. But answering the profound questions of life is not in the scientist's province. The ultimate meaning and purpose of life and the universe is a matter for the philosopher or theologian. Scientists can bring their expertise to help find the answers, indeed there sometimes is co-operation here, but a scientist is trained to answer the 'what' questions of life, not the 'why' questions.

What can science achieve?

What scientists are trying to do is to give a rational explanation of what happens in the universe. Each discipline investigates a particular aspect of the universe. Through careful observation, a scientist may reach certain conclusions, which he then formulates into a theory. If this is then tested by the community of scientists and found to be true to the way things are, it becomes an accepted 'law', a building-block used to explain what has happened, what does happen and what will happen. For example, when the sixteenth-century astronomer Johann Kepler observed the position of planets in the sky on successive nights, he was able to calculate the paths which the planets took. By establishing that they followed an elliptical path round the sun, he was able to formulate the laws which have formed the foundation of modern astronomy.

So scientific laws explain the nature of the physical universe. They can be used to predict its future behaviour. But can science explain everything? Given enough time, money and resources, there is no reason to suppose that all features of the physical universe could not be explained. If all there is to life is the physical then at this point we may as well say goodbye to any possible claim for God's existence. However, the Christian's awareness of God shows him that there is more to life than its physical side. There is also a spiritual dimension which scientific investigation is simply not equipped to explain or predict.

The 'God of the gaps' theory

Often in the past everything that went on in the natural world—winds and waves, planetary motion, weather, sickness—was attributed *directly* to God. Today most of these things are explained through geophysics, astronomy and microbiology.

As the methods of scientific enquiry got better established, it became obvious that most of those events previously thought of as mysterious could really be rationally explained. The areas where God had to be called upon to supply the explanation became fewer. God was being removed from 'the gaps' and squeezed out of the universe, which men could now explain in terms of natural laws.

This way of relating God to science was never sound, and it has caused a great deal of misunder-standing. Fortunately there is a better way.

The Christian knowledge of the world

Scientific knowledge is based on observation, enquiry and experiment. Christian knowledge (which in-cidentally many scientists also possess) is based on information supplied by God himself. It is a form of truth which we know because God has made it known. Within this one truth there are many truths. But basic to them all is the knowledge that there is a Creator of the Universe, who also sustains and upholds it. He is an eternal and infinite Spirit, invisible, but yet always present in his creation.

Scientific knowledge can neither prove nor disprove the existence of a Creator and Sustainer of the universe. It can only study what God has made and the way in which it is sustained and upheld. It gives us accurate knowledge of the physical universe, but is simply not the right map to guide us into the spiritual reality which is such a vital part of our lives within that universe.

The relation between scientific knowledge and faith-knowledge may become clearer if we think of it this way. You can describe a beautiful oil-painting quite accurately within the limits of its chemistry and the distribution of pigments on the canvas. Or the same painting may be described by someone else interested in its artistic design, brush-work and meaning. Both types of explanation —the material and the artistic—are correct and complete, but they do not overlap at all. They may be judged to be complementary alternatives. It is the same with the scientific and Christian descriptions of the physical world.

God cannot be quantified or measured. You cannot use a mathematical equation to locate him or define him. You might as well try to measure colour with a ruler or weigh radio waves. The equipment and judgements of

The advance of science has brought with it an understanding of life which finds it hard to believe what we cannot see and measure.

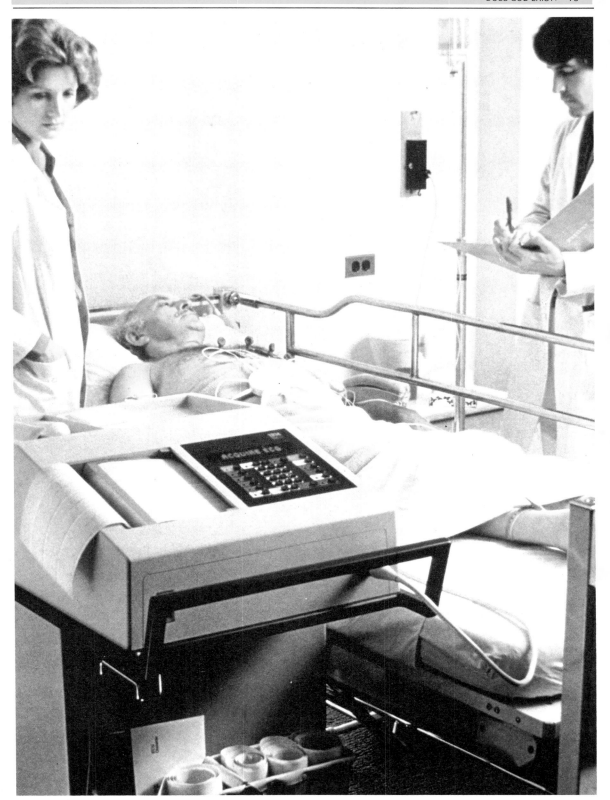

The New Testament recognizes that there are two ways of looking at the way we get our food. First, there is the natural law of growth: 'The soil itself makes the plants grow and bear fruit; first the tender stalk appears, then the ear, and finally the ear full of corn.'
Mark 4:28

Second, there is the invisible creative work of God: 'God created foods to be eaten.'
1 Timothy 4:3

science are not appropriate for analysing the spiritual world. Yet that very capacity for rational thought which is so necessary for the scientist is an ability given to humanity by God.

An open approach to God and science

The disciplines of science give us an ever-increasing knowledge of the beauty, complexity, regularity and mystery of the universe. Looked at with Christian eyes this rich store of explanation helps the believer to recognize the greatness of God in the immensity of the universe and the wisdom of God in its intricacies.

The scientist who sees his work as disproving God's existence is misguided. He has failed to understand either the extent of his own method or the nature of God. The believer who sees science as an activity in itself directly opposed to God's existence is equally misguided in his understanding of both science and God.

Science can never disprove or prove God's existence. But for those who believe in God it can provide a wonderful enrichment of faith.

9 DOES GOD EXIST?

GOD IN OTHER RELIGIONS

Many people think of the different religions of the world as merely different ways to a vague kind of God. They claim that just as there are many possible routes between London and Edinburgh or Paris or Rome (though not all of equal length or comfort), so there are many routes to God. What is important is the sincerity of the believer, not what he believes.

In the solar system (to take another example), the sun is in the centre and the earth, moon and planets travel round it. God, people say, is like the sun, with the various religions of the world revolving round him, attracted by him and receiving their light from him.

These two illustrations make sense only if the religions under consideration are similar—in their general view of God, for example. But in fact they are not. The view of God in traditional Hinduism is very different from that in Islam, Judaism and Christianity.

Hinduism

Hinduism is the religion of India and to a lesser degree of Sri Lanka, Bali and Malaysia. In recent times it has had a great attraction for young people in Western society.

The teaching of the Vedas (the earliest Hindu holy books) knows nothing of a divine Spirit who relates to people. God is Brahman, the true absolute—unknown, abstract. The whole universe proceeds from Brahman as a spider's web flows out of the spider itself. Brahman is everywhere but not one can see it, touch, smell or taste it, or know its presence. All human attempts to describe Brahman fail and no moral

qualities may be ascribed to it. It is neither loving nor unloving, good nor bad.

Alongside this philosophical view of the essence of things, there is the practice, so fascinating to visitors to India, of worshipping the gods and goddesses of popular Hinduism. If all village deities of India are numbered, the figure is 330 million! Although this belief in one absolute Brahman and many local deities seems contradictory to Westerners, it poses no problem for the typical devotee of one or other of the gods of Hinduism. The deities are all absorbed into Brahman and each god or goddess is a manifestation of ultimate reality.

This brief summary shows how little correspondence there is between the belief in one living God, who is the final (personal) reality, and belief in an impersonal absolute, of which the thousands of deities are merely manifestations. In some modern, sophisticated expressions of Hinduism, especially among intellectuals, the idea of Brahman is developed in such a way as to make it more like a personal, living God. But such developments cannot be called authentic Hinduism.

Judaism, Islam and Christianity

Since Judaism, Islam and Christianity all trace their view of God to the revelation made to Abraham and Moses, and since all three religions confess that there is only one God, obviously they must worship the same God. And so the question which arises is: How do their views of God differ, and why do Christians claim that they alone have the right way to understand God and to worship him?

● **Islam**, the religion of a book (the Qur'an), is wholly committed to a God who is outside and beyond our lives. The Lord is one and has no partner, no wife and no children; he is totally different from his creatures. Converts are enrolled on the confession of the creed: 'There is no deity but God and Muhammad is the prophet of God.' God is both above his creatures and

Muslims are called to prayer by the muezzin. Mounting a minaret of the mosque he cries in a penetrating voice: 'God is most great. I testify that there is no God but Allah. I testify that Muhammad is God's apostle. Come to prayer, come to security. God is most great.'

One of the statements made by the worshippers is: 'God is One, the eternal God; begetting not and unbegotten; none is equal to him.'

Recited by pious Jews each morning and evening, the Shema is found in the Law of Moses (Deuteronomy 6, 4–5). 'Israel, remember this! The Lord—and the Lord alone—is our God. Love the Lord your God with all your heart, with all your soul and with all your strength . . .

For Christians Jesus, as God become man, has the unique and central place. The opening sentences of the letter to the Hebrews bring this out: 'In the past God spoke to our ancestors many times and in many places through the prophets, but in these last days he has spoken to us through his Son. He is the one through whom God created the universe, the one whom God has chosen to possess all things at the end. He reflects the brightness of God's glory and the exact likeness of God's own being, sustaining the universe with his powerful word. After achieving forgiveness for the sins of mankind, he sat down in heaven at the right-hand side of God, the Supreme Power'.

different from them in kind. Whatever his creatures think or do, it cannot affect him, for he is wholly independent of them. His will is supreme and cannot be changed. The right relation to him is that of submission—the word *Islam* means submission. Everything is pre-ordained and nothing happens which Allah (God) did not plan. Allah is supremely the God of justice and order, whose law must be obeyed and whose will is final.

Islam has little to say about the grace, compassion and love of God for those who need his help. It does not promise communion with

God in worship, for worship is simply a service which Allah has commanded.

● **Judaism**, like Islam is also the religion of a book. That book is the Hebrew Bible, or the Old Testament as Christians call it, on which much of the Qur'an is based. The essence of Judaism is contained in the *Shema*, which is often recited in Jewish worship (see below). This statement of faith affirms that there is one living God who is to be loved and obeyed and whose laws must be taught to the children. Judaism, like Islam, rejects all forms of idol-worship and teaches that God is holy, just and uplifted. Yet, unlike Islam, it teaches that God becomes involved in the world: he loves his people, comes to their help, and is willing to change his mind if they respond to his word and will. In worship there is genuine communion between God and men. Not only does he send prophets to speak his words to them, but he will send his specially chosen servant, the Messiah, who will bring into being the kingdom of God.

The major difference between Islam and Judaism on the one hand, and *Christianity* on the other, is that for Christians Jesus is much more than a prophet; he is God become man who lived in Palestine as the Jewish Messiah.

Islam accepts Jesus as a prophet. Judaism regards him as a prophet who claimed falsely to be the Messiah. Christianity is based on the fact that Jesus is more than simply God's final revelation and self-disclosure to men. Christians deny nothing about God which Jews teach; but they claim that the full, complete picture of God is only found by looking to Jesus. In him God is fully revealed as Saviour, Redeemer, Friend and Guide.

When Jesus, God become man, completed his task and left the earth his work was continued by the Holy Spirit, God in action, who lives in the hearts of humble believers and represents Jesus in the world. This is why Christians talk about God as Father, Son and Holy Spirit. They worship only one God, but they encounter this one God in the

A Sadhu meditates in a yoga position. Are all religions equally effective routes to God?

Father (whom Jews and Muslims know as God), in the Son (Jesus, God become man) and in the Holy Spirit (God working in the world and dwelling in human hearts). So they have a view of God which, in summary, is One in Three and Three in One. (This 'trinitarian' view is more fully explained in the section, *God the three-in-one.*)

9 DOES GOD EXIST?

CAN GOD BE PROVED?

If there is one supreme God, Lord of all, you would think we human beings, whom he has created, would be fully and vividly aware of his existence. But apparently we are not. So the question is often asked of believers, 'Can you prove the existence of God?'

People who ask this question have not usually given thought to what they mean by 'prove'. There are two basic types of proof. First there is proof which is based on experience. I can prove that there are twenty cows in the field by taking you into the field with me to count them. But there is also proof based on a process of reasoning or rational demonstration. I can prove that a thief came to my home by pointing to the footprints in the garden, the forced lock in the door, the footprints on the carpet, the fingerprints on the cupboard handle, the absence of my silver and the scattered papers on my desk. All this evidence, taken together, leads me to conclude I have been burgled.

Now if God is an infinite, eternal Being, who is Spirit and thus invisible, he cannot be seen as I can see the cows in the field. So if the existence of God is to be proved, then it can only be by evidence. This has to be found and brought together so that the deduction from the evidence is reasonable—as with the evidence for the thief. The level of certainty at which this method arrives is not absolute; it is possible that the evidence for the supposed thief's visit to my house can be explained some other way (as readers of crime stories will know). So arguments for God's existence cannot be totally conclusive; rather they provide large and broad hints that he *most probably* exists. They cannot stand alone. To be forceful and compelling they

have to be accompanied by a genuine experience of the presence and reality of God.

Here are three different arguments for the existence of God. Each of them is well-known and has often been used.

The argument from a First Cause

The things I see as I look around my study—table, desk, chair, books and so on—are not there by any absolute necessity. They might well never have existed or been placed there. All were made by human beings using material made by others or taken from 'nature'. And even in nature the existence of the tree (from which came the wood for the table and the pulp to make paper) is due to the fact that a seed germinated and began to grow. Behind the existence of the tree is a long story of causation. Its existence is not self-explanatory. It owes its existence and meaning to causes outside itself. In fact it is the same with everything in the world. The final explanation for anything is not found in itself. Nothing exists of necessity. So everything that exists points beyond itself to a series of causes and they in turn point to an ultimate and final Cause. There must be a First Cause from which all causation is derived. Such a First Cause must be the source of growth, change and movement. Further, to be the source of all causes, this First Cause must be living and have a mind. In other words, the First Cause is 'the living God'.

The argument from design

Suppose that you have never seen a transistor radio before and you find one as you walk down a lonely path. You examine it and note how all the parts work harmoniously together to produce sounds. And so you conclude that it was made by an intelligent being for a particular purpose (which you may or may not realize). Much the same applies to our world. The study of each part and of the whole may suggest that it was made by an intelligent being for a particular purpose. Whether you study the smallest plant, the human

The psalmist sees atheism as evidence of stupidity: 'Fools say to themselves, "There is no God".' *Psalms 14:1; 53:1*

Though he did not find it wholly convincing as an argument for God's existence, Immanuel Kant (1724–1803), one of Europe's greatest philosophers, said the following about the argument from design: 'This proof always deserves to be mentioned with respect. It is the oldest, the clearest and the most accordant with the common reason of mankind. It enlivens the study of nature, just as it itself derives its existence and gains ever new vigour from that source. It suggests ends and purposes, where our observation would not have detected them by itself, and extends our knowledge of nature by means of the guiding-concept of a special unity, the principle of which is outside nature. This knowledge . . . so strengthens the belief in the supreme Author of nature that the belief acquires the force of an irresistible conviction.'

body, the solar system or the wings of a bird you conclude that there is design, often intricate and complex design.

Since design is found in all things and everywhere, and since all things appear to fit into one overall design, the logical step is to suggest that there is a supreme intelligence behind the universe—the great Designer. This Designer has designed and produced life and minds and so must himself be living and have a mind. In other words the Designer is 'the living God'.

The argument from conscience and moral law

Whether occasionally or often, we all have the feeling that 'I ought to do something'. On such occasions the human conscience is working, making the person feel he should do what his mind tells him is right. The duty may be repaying a debt, helping an infirm or elderly person, apologizing for harm done or getting to work on time. Most of us also feel ashamed of ourselves from time to time for not doing what we should have done. People have argued that this universal sense of duty and obligation points to a supernatural reality from whom all moral values stem, for such values cannot be explained in materialistic terms. In other words, conscience is the voice of God, who is the source of moral values.

Another aspect of this argument points to the powerful claim which moral values have upon a person's life. Such values as telling the truth, loving and respecting people, or preserving the sanctity of life do not seem to be the product of our own minds. They face us as something outside and beyond ourselves. They are normally expressed in laws—not to lie, steal, kill and so on—which appear objective, belonging to the nature of the universe. So people have argued that the presence of moral law points to a source of morality, to God, who is the Moral Governor of the universe.

Whether or not these or similar arguments are compelling is closely related to the state of mind of the person who studies them. A sceptic will probably remain a sceptic while a person who wants to believe in God may be helped by them to a true faith.

In fact the writers of the Bible never really tried to *prove* the existence of God. They wrote what they knew of God and his ways and the only kind of proof for God they describe is proof that he, the living God they believe in, is superior to the idols of the heathen. They are moved by the beauty, design and order of the world to worship God. But they are also disturbed by all the *dis*order in the world, as many people are today. In particular, the presence of suffering is a real test of their faith. It is only when Jesus Christ became so fully identified with the pain and evil in people's lives that this problem began to come into more positive focus. (See the section *God and suffering*.)

10 WHAT IS GOD LIKE?

TALKING ABOUT GOD

When they speak of their belief, Christians often seem to use language in rather an odd way. On the one hand they claim that God is an eternal, infinite Spirit, while on the other they apparently feel no particular problem when they describe God walking in the garden of Eden, having a Son, speaking to human beings, even repenting and laughing. Can an eternal Spirit walk, talk, repent, and laugh, not to mention be a father?

At first sight, and certainly to believers, Bible passages such as the twenty-third psalm or the Lord's Prayer seem clear and straightforward. Yet their meaning is not so obvious if they are read in what we may call an everyday, earthbound sense. Take the Lord's Prayer: 'Our Father' (but not our parent) 'in heaven' (though not among the galaxies) ... 'may your kingdom come' (yet not as an earthly kingdom) ... 'give us today the food we need' (which we shall buy or make) ... etc. The psalm, with its talk of shepherds and tables, contains even greater difficulties, if taken in an earthbound sense. Yet to people of faith such statements apparently cause little or no difficulty.

Special language

Certainly some religious language is used in a plain, literal sense—as in such statements as 'Jesus was crucified under Pontius Pilate', or 'the apostles placed their hands on them'. And religious language has many of the forms which everyday language has: there is poetry, prose, metaphor and allegory.

However, even recognizing that religious language has many points of contact with everyday speech, it is still an odd type of language. The Bible, along with hymns and popular literature, describes God as though he were a kind of SuperMan. This kind of description is given the technical name of 'anthropomorphism' (from *anthropos*, 'man' and *morphe*, 'shape'). It should not be dismissed as primitive. It is actually a convenient use of language, for it uses the very words with which we are familiar, instead of trying to invent new ones, which no one else would understand. Further, and this is important, it flows out of religious experience and is the natural way to relate and describe that experience.

So it is possible to be a good Christian and not be conscious of the oddity of the language used, because it seems to describe so well the experience of God we enjoy. There is in fact a variety of explanations of how religious language works. Here, in brief, is the explanation which Christians have offered most often since medieval times.

The language of analogy

Believers use such words as good, great, loving, powerful and wise both of human beings and of God. They refer to God and to individual men as father, son, king, shepherd, bridegroom and lord. Does each of these words have precisely the same meaning when used of God and of a man? The answer must be 'no', for God is not good or a father in exactly the same way as a man is good and a father.

So does this mean that the words 'good' and 'father' are used with several completely unrelated meanings (just as a 'bat' can be what I use to hit a ball, or a creature that lives in an old barn)? Again the answer must be 'no', for if there is no relation then language about God is meaningless and a waste of time.

We call these two ways of using words 'univocal' and 'equivocal' respectively. But there is a middle way between these two—the 'analogical'. This explanation of how language about God can be meaningful depends on there being

The Bible recognizes that our best thoughts and words about God still fall far short of the perfection of God's thoughts:
'My thoughts,' says the Lord, 'are not like yours, and my ways are different from yours. As high as the heavens are above the earth so high are my ways and thoughts above yours.'
Isaiah 55:8-9

'How great are God's riches! How deep are his wisdom and knowledge! Who can explain his decisions? Who can understand his ways? As the Scripture says "Who knows the mind of the Lord? Who is able to give him advice?" . . . For all things were created by him, and all things exist through him and for him. To God be the glory for ever! Amen.'
Romans 11:33-35

From the greatest thinker of the early Christian centuries: 'More true than our speech about God is our thinking of him, and more true than our thinking is his Being.'
Augustine

a definite relation between God and man. And there is such a relationship. It is found in the idea of God as the Creator and man as the creature, which is made even more specific in the picture of man made in the image of God. That is, human beings mirror in some minute way the character of God their Creator.

An analogy is a relation between two things or persons which may be called a likeness. There are two kinds which are particularly helpful to the Christian looking at his language about God. The first is the kind found in the statements, 'John is healthy' and 'The coastal town is healthy'. Only John is truly healthy; the town is healthy in a derivative sense because its climate and geographical position make health possible. Therefore, if God is Creator and I am the creature, he possesses wisdom, love and goodness in their perfection and fullness while I possess them in a derivative sense. They belong truly to him, but being made in his image

these aspects of his character can be found in me.

The second type of analogy is the kind we meet in such statements as, 'What a clever dog you've got!' and 'Albert Einstein was a very clever man'. Here the analogy is that the dog is clever in a way appropriate for a dog to be clever (he can carry the shopping bag in his teeth), while Einstein is clever in a way appropriate for a top-level scientist to be clever (he stated the theory of relativity). Therefore in language about God and man the believer is claiming that God is wise, good and loving in a way appropriate for an eternal, infinite Spirit to be wise, good and loving; a human being is wise, good and loving in a way appropriate for a finite creature to be so.

If these two types of analogy are put together then it is a proper claim that, because God is Creator and man is his creature, language by men about God is meaningful. Of course it does not mean that believers can provide an exhaustive description of God. It means that while there can be reliable information about God, the character and being of God always remain beyond our best thoughts and most accurate descriptions.

GOD AND THE UNIVERSE

No one was surprised when the first Russian astronauts did not see God in their space travels. Christians hold that God cannot be seen with the human eye since he is eternal, infinite Spirit.

Of course our concept of the size of the universe has changed over the centuries. Christians have been as dependent as others on the latest research in cosmology. So today the universe is a much vaster place than it was in medieval or ancient times. To talk in terms of 'light-years' is now commonplace.

But however much our understanding of the size and nature of the universe may change the Christian view of the relationship of God to the world stays substantially the same. What has happened is that the reality of God has had to be reconciled to the reality of an apparently expanding universe. This has forced new questions into view, such as, 'If there is life on other planets did God/will God become man there too?' It has made theologians more careful in their use of language to describe God and his world. Yet we need to appreciate even more clearly today than before that the cosmologist's questions are not the same as those asked by the Christian believer.

Knowing that God really exists, the believer wants to know what is his relationship to the universe. The traditional Christian answer goes like this:

The Dumb-bell nebula, one of the beautiful spiral nebulae, light-years away in space. The vastness of the universe has often made people feel insignificant. If God exists and is ruler of these immensities, how can he be closely interested in the inhabitants of one tiny speck in a particular galaxy?

God is outside the universe

A potter makes a vase; a carpenter makes a table; a painter paints a picture and the old clockmaker makes a grandfather-clock. In other words, what is made is distinct from the person who makes it. So God, if he is the Creator of the universe, must be distinct from it. As Creator of time and space, he must be beyond the limits of them—the word for this is *transcendent*.

But from what did God make the universe? Christians have always maintained that he made it out of nothing—that he created the basic atoms, molecules and electrons, and with them fashioned the universe. 'Creation out of nothing' is not a scientific theory but a statement of faith based on the teaching of the Bible. The concerns of the scientist and the believer are quite different. Christians affirm that God created everything. Scientists, some of whom of course are believers, study what the creation is made of and how it develops. But though these concerns are different, they do not have to be in conflict. They can be complementary.

Only a God who is transcendent can be the Creator and Sustainer of the vast universe we know. He cannot in any way be dependent on the universe, because the universe is wholly dependent on him. This is why Christians believe that God is outside and beyond the universe.

God is present in the universe

Although God is beyond the universe, he is not absent from it. The creation is not a clock which God made, wound up and now leaves ticking. Nor is humanity like a gang of tenant farmers on an estate with an absentee landlord. The transcendent God is present in his creation—the word for this is *immanent*. And he is present in certain very real and definite ways.

● God is there in the world he has made. His creative mind is to be seen in the beauty and order of the

The Bible contains very many passages which reflect God's transcendence, immanence and transparence:

Paul, the apostle: 'There is one God and Father of all mankind, who is Lord of all, works through all, and is in all.'
Ephesians 4:6

The prophet Isaiah: 'I am the high and holy God who lives for ever. I live in a high and holy place, but I also live with people who are humble and repentant, so that I can restore their confidence and hope.'
Isaiah 57:15

God's presence in the universe is eloquently portrayed by the Psalmist:
> Where could I go to escape from you?
> Where could I get away from your presence?
> If I went up to heaven, you would be there;
> if I lay down in the world of the dead, you would be there.

The idea of God holding the universe in being comes out in an illustration used by Professor Donald MacKay:
'Take the kind of television tennis game that modern electronics has made possible, where players can control the movement of various objects appearing on a TV screen by means of the knobs and switches on a "black box" in their own living room. Here the "ball" and the "bat" are dynamically stable patches of light held in being by a coherent succession of control signals, and moved around the screen by changing the timing of those control signals. But in this case what we are watching is not a representation of the real world as seen through some distant television camera. It is an *artificially created* scene, in which every object owes both its existence and its motions directly to the sustaining programme generated by the black box, as modulated by the players. Not only the contents of this synthetic world, but its laws of motion too, have dynamic rather than static ability. They are perfectly stable, for just as long as the generating programme is stable. But at the flick of a switch the contents of the synthetic world can alter completely

universe, in much the same way as a composer can be heard in the music he writes. It bears his characteristic hallmark. The world is the way it is because it is God who made it.

● There is one more way in which God is immanent in the world. It is a more particular, visible and felt sense than the other He was present in Jesus of Nazareth, who showed God's nature with unique clarity as he lived, loved and worshipped with exactly the character of God himself.

● But he is also there in another way. God so made the universe that it is totally dependent on his power at every moment to stay intact and in motion. God can exist without the universe but the universe cannot exist without him. He is in it as its upholder, sustainer and energizer, giving it continued existence and operating the laws of nature. So, for instance, season follows on season and the plant grows from the seed.

God is simultaneously outside the universe (transcendent) and inside the universe (immanent). He can be both inside and outside at one and the same time because he is the Creator of the universe and infinite, eternal Spirit.

Sometimes a positive truth is made clearer by pointing out what is denied and rejected. Christians have denied:

● Deism, the view that God is Creator of the universe but not actively involved in its present life,

● Pantheism, the view that God is everything and everything is God.

Deism exalts transcendence and Pantheism exalts immanence. The orthodox Christian affirms both the transcendence and immanence of God.

10 WHAT IS GOD LIKE?

GOD THE THREE-IN-ONE

Preachers have made many attempts to explain what God as a Trinity means. These are some of the popular illustrations I have heard. The three-leaf clover has one leaf, which is really three. H_2O comes in three forms—ice, water and steam. The triangle is a three-sided figure. The problem with these illustrations is that they are physical rather than personal.

In fact, simple illustrations rarely help people to understand the Christian teaching that God is One, yet One in Three and Three in One. And in many cases these illustrations give a wrong picture of what God is like.

Why do Christians believe that God is simultaneously One and Three?

To answer this question we need to put the argument in two stages. First, why Christians believe God is One, and then why they believe he is Three in One.

The belief that there is one God, Creator of the universe, and Lord of all, is common to Judaism, Islam and Christianity. It is a fundamental principle of the Old Testament, which opens with the claim that 'In the beginning God created the universe', and contains what Jews call the *shema*: 'The Lord our God is one Lord and you shall love him with all your heart, soul and strength.' This deeply held conviction is continued in the New Testament, being repeated and affirmed by Jesus and his apostles.

The unity of God means not only that there is (mathematically speaking) one God and one alone; it also means that as an eternal, infinite Spirit, there is a perfect unity within his being, thoughts and actions. That is, a perfect harmony exists in everything that he is, thinks, says and does.

From where, then, did the idea of God as Trinity come? Certainly the early Christians and apostles did not invent this teaching in order to complicate life and thought for later Christians. It came as the inevitable result of two things—first, reaction to the person and teaching of Jesus, and then experience of fellowship with God.

The disciples of Jesus identified 'the Father' to whom Jesus prayed and of whom he taught (as in the Lord's Prayer, 'Our Father ...') with the God of Abraham, Moses and Elijah, the God of the Jews. This was a sensible thing to do and Jesus encouraged it. However, they also came overwhelmingly to realize that God was revealed in Jesus; that they encountered the living God directly and unmistakably in Jesus, their teacher from Nazareth. (See further the answer to the question *Is Jesus really God?*). They were also conscious of the clear teaching of Jesus (carefully recorded in John's Gospel, chapters 14–16) about a living, spiritual Person who would come to them from the Father and be with them, taking the place of Jesus after his resurrection and ascension. Therefore they knew God as Father, experienced God as Son and would experience God through the Holy Spirit. One God was known by them in three modes of being.

This interpretation of the teaching of Jesus was confirmed in the experience of the first Christians as they met for fellowship and worship and as they sought to tell the world of Jesus and his love. In their lives they knew the presence of the Holy Spirit and in his power they both worshipped the Father in the name of the Son and had fellowship with one another in the love of God. They believed that their salvation, and their hope for eternal life, were wholly based upon the work of Father, Son and Holy Spirit for them. They did not provide in the New Testament a reasoned explanation of *how* God was real to them in three modes. What they did

do was to provide a testimony of how they experienced the *reality* of God as Father, Son and Holy Spirit.

The orthodox Christian teaching

The actual attempt to provide a reasoned explanation of how God is One yet Three was made by two important church synods or councils three centuries after the resurrection of Christ. These were held at Nicea (325) and Constantinople (381). Not that these synods wanted to provide carefully contrived theological formulae. They would have preferred to keep to the dynamic, if not precise, language of the New Testament. But they felt obliged to state what they held to be the truth about God because of the presence in the churches of what they believed were false views and wrong doctrines. Their teaching is found in what we call the *Nicene Creed*, recited in many churches today. It is also found in a longer and even more precise form in the *Athanasian Creed* (= Quicunque Vult) which was composed in Italy about AD 500.

Today, committed Christians experience the living God as did the first Christians. They experience him as One and yet as Father, Son and Holy Spirit. They may not fully understand it. They simply follow the teaching of the New Testament. It is important to do so, and make the effort to understand this doctrine, at a time when there are so many cults and sects around who deny the Trinity.

Here is the orthodox Christian teaching:

● There is only one living God.
● The Father exists eternally as God.
● The Son exists eternally as God.
● The Holy Spirit exists eternally as God.
● The Father, Son and Holy Spirit share equally in one Godhead.

Two technical words have traditionally been used in the explanation of the Trinity. They are *Person*, which means 'a mode of being', and *Substance* (or 'Being'), which describes that deity and godhead which all three Persons (Father, Son and Holy Spirit) share. So Christians believe in One God known as Three Persons who equally share the one divine Being and Substance.

Each part of this belief is important. If a person comes to hold, say, that God the Father, Son and Holy Spirit do not equally share in the one Godhead, and that only the Father is truly God, his belief is no longer really a Christian one. It has been a common minority viewpoint over the centuries and is propagated today by Jehovah's Witnesses.

10 WHAT IS GOD LIKE?

IS JESUS REALLY GOD?

Jesus of Nazareth has always been a fascinating figure. He still attracts the attention of young and old, poets and philosophers, song-writers and film-makers, rich and poor, brown, yellow, black and white. Interest in him is high in East and West, North and South, developed and developing countries, whether communist or democratic. He stands firmly in history but somehow he is beyond and above history. His appeal comes over the centuries but is also a contemporary appeal; he seems to be timeless. His life was exemplary. His teaching is beautiful. He showed us a life full of purpose, meaning and inner harmony. He was perfect.

Christians are glad to hear all this, but they want to say more. They want to say that in Jesus we find God. In a way beyond our full understanding, God became a human being as Jesus of Nazareth. This happened because God loves us. He wants to come right where we are and help us.

Why do Christians believe that Jesus is God?

One thing is sure. The early Christians did not invent the teaching that Jesus is the eternal Son of God just to gain a following. It was something they were forced to acknowledge and confess by the weight of evidence in its favour. Their Jewish background had not

Song, dance, silence – Christians use many different ways to worship Jesus as the divine Son of God. But was he really more than a very good man?

prepared them for such a conclusion.

Certainly Jesus was extraordinary. The Galilean crowds were amazed at his authoritative teaching and the way he ministered to the sick and outcasts. The disciples shared this sense of wonder, but they went further. They came to acknowledge Jesus as the promised Saviour of Israel; he was the 'Messiah', chosen by God and empowered with the Holy Spirit. Of him the ancient prophets had spoken and for him the Jews had longed.

When Jesus was crucified as a criminal and then buried in a hillside tomb, the disciples lost their faith. But they regained it when they met Jesus, who had risen from the dead. Then, as the risen Jesus met them and taught them they became sure he was the long-expected Messiah, promised in the Old Testament. And when he permanently left them (in what we call the ascension), their faith was not disturbed. They were confident he was alive in heaven for ever. They received the personal gift of the Holy Spirit in their lives. By this presence they knew that Jesus was with them wherever they went. So, in the name of Jesus and the power of the Holy Spirit, they preached the good news of his resurrection, healed the sick, made converts and formed churches. (This exciting story is found in the Acts of the Apostles.)

As they lived and preached for Jesus, experiencing his power and presence, the leaders of the disciples recalled what Jesus had taught them. They meditated on some of the deep teaching he had given about himself. They remembered overhearing Jesus pray: 'I have shown your glory on earth; I have finished the work you gave me to do. Father! Give me the glory in your presence now, the same glory I had with you before the world was made.' This kind of teaching made them realize that, while Jesus was certainly the Messiah, he was more than the Messiah. That is, he could only be the Saviour of the whole world if he were more than a mere mortal man. Only the Son of God

FROM THE NEW TESTAMENT:

Peter, the leader of the inner circle of the followers of Jesus: 'You are the Messiah, the Son of the living God.' *Matthew 16:16*

'Messiah'—or 'Christ'—is the name of the Saviour and Leader for whom the Jews prayed. Peter says Jesus is this Saviour. 'Son' is sometimes a title for the Messiah in the Old Testament, but it also contains hints of the intimate relation and union between the Father and Jesus.

Jesus told his disciple, Thomas: 'I am the way, the truth and the life; no one comes to the Father except by me.' *John 14:6*

Jesus is claiming that he alone can open the way to a relationship between human beings and the Father. This is because, as the disciples were later to recognize, Jesus is both God and man. As such he brings God to man and man to God.

John, at the beginning of his Gospel: 'The Word became a human being, and, full of grace and truth, lived among us. We beheld his glory, the glory which he received as the Father's only Son.' *John 1:14*

Earlier he had stated that 'Before the world was created, the Word already existed; he was with God and he was the same as God' (1:1)

In the Greek language 'Word' (=Logos) was a common term to describe the meaning of the universe. Here John has personalized this idea to show that the true key to the meaning of the universe is in the eternal Son of God who became man.

Peter again, in his sermon on the day of Pentecost: 'This Jesus, whom you crucified, is the one that God has made Lord and Messiah.' *Acts 2:36*

'God has raised this very Jesus from death, and we are all witnesses to this fact. He has been raised to the right hand side of God his Father.' *2:32*

The resurrection of Jesus was the foundation of the good news preached by the first Christians.

becoming man could in fact truly achieve what Jesus had achieved.

So when they wrote their letters to the churches, the leaders taught that Jesus was Messiah and also eternal Son of God. The apostle Paul loved to describe Jesus as 'the Lord'. This was a title used not only of the Roman Emperor but of God in the Old Testament. It was Paul's way of affirming that Jesus was more than man; he was divine.

How can Jesus be both God and man at the same time?

To understand that Jesus is an extraordinary man is easy enough. To understand that Jesus is God in a human body is rather difficult. But to understand that Jesus is *both* God (that is truly God) and man (that is truly man) is very hard.

We need to be clear that the early Christians were not keen to cause intellectual headaches to

those who followed them. Most Christians of the first century were content to accept what the apostles said about Jesus and get on with the task of serving him in the Roman Empire. Yet eventually the difficult questions had to be faced, particularly when obviously false teaching was heard inside the churches.

At certain times the Christian church had to insist that Jesus was in the fullest sense a human being—not a phantom or a ghost. At others it had to insist that Jesus was in the fullest sense God. One famous occasion when the divinity of Christ was clearly stated was at the Council of Nicea (325), presided over by Emperor Constantine. False teachers had been saying that although Jesus was truly a man, he was not God become man: rather he was a spiritual being from heaven taking human form. So the Council stated in clear and emphatic terms that whatever divinity the Father has the Son has the same; if the Father is God so is Jesus. The words of the Creed of Nicea have been recited in church services since that time.

It was not surprising that much attention was also given in the church to finding the best way to state that Jesus is both perfect God and perfect man in one reality at all times. Eventually a formula was adopted by the Council of Chalcedon in 451, and this has guided the thinking of the church ever since.

In principle, God and man are compatible. Since God created human beings, who are the crown of the creation, there is a special and unique relation between God and man. The Bible describes this in terms of man being made in the image and likeness of God. Yet, in Jesus, God and man were united in a much more intimate way than human beings relate to God as their Creator. The nature of this union defies final definition. What the New Testament presents is one living reality, Jesus. Christians confess that he is always and certainly God and always and certainly man. He is not like Jekyll and Hyde and he is not schizophrenic. He is truly God and truly man perfectly joined as one living person.

11 IS GOD INVOLVED?

CREATION AND EVOLUTION

'The book of Genesis says that God made the world, and made human beings as a special part of creation. But scientists have proved that we are descended from apes. So the Bible must be wrong.' This kind of statement is still made today and has a long history.

The debate between scientists and theologians has in the past been extremely bitter. The controversy over evolution illustrates this. It began in earnest after the publication of Darwin's epic book, *On the Origin of the Species by means of Natural Selection*, in 1859. In the following year the traditionalist Bishop Wilberforce and the agonostic Professor T. H. Huxley were at loggerheads. In a public debate at Oxford, Wilberforce attacked Darwin's ideas, which he thought were contrary to the Bible, making man of no more importance than an animal. For if man were likened to a ape how could he be made in the image of God?

The controversy has continued and still has much heat left in it, especially in parts of the US. Today, however, Darwin's basic ideas are accepted by the majority of professional Christian biologists. They apparently find no insuperable difficulty in holding both to the theory of evolution and to what they believe is the truth about God and man taught in the Bible.

So does the theory of evolution contradict the belief that God is the Creator of the universe and that human beings are a special part of that creation?

Darwin's teaching

Charles Darwin brought together a mass of information which convinced him that life has evolved over millions of years. His attempt to collect all the evidence was the first scientific account of the facts. No other satisfactory explanation of all the facts he presented has yet been proposed. His theory of how evolution occurred may be set out as follows:

● **The struggle for existence** In nature there is a struggle for existence in animals and plants. Normally the number of individuals of a species in a given area or community does not vary greatly. This implies that the progeny which survive to become mature breeding individuals is much the same in number as those which die. Yet generally speaking the capacity for reproduction of a species is greater than this—plants produce thousands of seeds of which only a few reach maturity.

● **Variation** Individuals in a species—human beings for example—differ from one another and are not identical. Generally the variations between individuals are passed on to the next generation in reproduction. Tall parents normally produce tall children.

● **Survival of the fittest** If there is an intense struggle for existence in their natural environment among individuals of a species, those which are best fitted for that environment survive to maturity and breed. The particular characteristics which enabled them to survive will be passed on to their offspring. This process is liable to continue and a species will become better adapted to its environment.

● **Natural selection** Over a long period of time the environment in which any species lives will not be stable but will change. As it does so, the characteristics which best fit the individual to the changed environment will be selected (according to the principle of survival of the fittest) and the species will change. The environment will not change for all of a given species in the same way, and so in particular areas a new species may evolve through adaptation to that new environment.

Darwin thought of evolution as a

slow, continuous process. He saw natural selection operating on the small, inheritable variations found between the individuals of a species as they undergo intense competition. As would be expected, some of Darwin's ideas have been modified, especially because of greater knowledge of genetics, but in essence they are still accepted by biologists.

Christian teaching

Christian teaching begins from the position that God, the eternal and infinite Spirit, is the Creator and Upholder of the universe. Therefore everything in the universe ultimately originates from him. He is responsible for all the matter, all the processes and all the phenomena which make up the universe. The existence of species, and any relationship which they have to each other, therefore results from his creative acts.

Human beings are part of the creation, but a unique part. Only humans, with their mental, moral and spiritual capabilities and qualities, are able to have meaningful fellowship and communion with their Creator. They are made 'in his image'. They can also use their free will to reject their Creator and follow their own ideas and will. When they do this, they forgo fellowship with God.

Different but not contradictory

We are all familiar with different but not contradictory statements of what are the same thing. London seen from the window of a jumbo jet as it flies westwards along the Thames towards Heathrow Airport looks very different from London viewed from the deck of a pleasure steamer going in the same direction on the river. Each gives a true but different perspective on London.

From the viewpoint of the biologist the ape and the human being are very similar. Their anatomy and physiology are much the same and what they have in common, biologically, is much greater than their differences. A relationship between them seems probable, and evolutionary theory seeks to explain this by arguing

The basic Christian position: 'It is by faith that we understand that the universe was created by God's word, so that what can be seen was made out of what cannot be seen.'
Hebrews 11:3

The special place of humanity in the created order: 'God created man in his own image, in the image of God created he him; male and female created he them.'
Genesis 1:27

'Look at the birds flying around; they do not sow seeds, gather a harvest and put it in barns; yet your Father in heaven takes care of them! Aren't you worth much more than the birds?'
Jesus, in Matthew 6:26

A quotation from a collection of writings by scientists who are Christians:
'If Christians are to accept the modern world of scientific inquiry and technology, they must learn to think of God's providence as working through and within the finite relations of things to one another and not . . . alongside of and separate from those relations . . . In regard to origins, God works through all the secondary causes that have played their part in the development of life on earth. Science studies by its empirical methods these finite causes— in the case of evolution, genetic mutations and natural selection—in the workings of which religious faith discerns, however dimly, the mysterious activity of God's providence. And just as the events of history or of an individual's life seem from the outside to be "random", yet in them the eye of faith can discover the workings of God, so the processes of natural development seem to the inquiries of science to be entirely random, yet to the mind of faith they manifest the mystery of God's creative and providential will.'

that both evolved from the same biological ancestor.

From the viewpoint of the anthropologist interested in culture (how people live together, what customs they have) the difference between apes and humans is much greater, although there are similarities.

From the viewpoint of the Christian as a person of faith a further dimension is added. For the teaching of the Bible shows that apes and humans are radically different. This is because the comparison is made, not at the biological or even the anthropological level, but at the level of their inner nature and relationship with God. Christians believe that apes are purely animals having no spiritual dimension, whereas human beings are made 'in the image of God', having a moral and spiritual nature which finds satisfaction only in communion with God our Creator.

The theory of evolution seeks to explain the relationships between the different forms of life and the process of development from simpler to more complex forms. Christian faith expresses knowledge of what may be termed final, ultimate causes of origin and development, which cannot be investigated by the methods of the biologist. Thus they can be complementary accounts, the one telling us *how* and the other telling us *why* and *who*.

Those who accept the theory of evolution and also believe the Bible to be true, see the early chapters of Genesis as teaching fundamental truths about God and his relationship to the world in a form which would have been just as meaningful for people living in the time of Moses as it is for us today. These chapters contain principles which are always true about God and his relationship to our world. The form in which the truths are expressed has to be recognized as an ancient type of literature; it was not intended to be 'scientific'.

That the theory of evolution may one day be modified or even abandoned in favour of another theory is possible. The scientists' knowledge, based on investigation and enquiry, is never complete. Revision of theories is continuous. The Christian, in contrast, bases his beliefs about God and the universe on what he believes God has revealed, recorded in the Bible. His faith-knowledge is based on principles which he regards as being always true. Changes in scientific opinions need never undermine his faith.

Evolution and the idea of 'the fall'

What Christians call sin involves wrong relationships with God and his creation. To live independently of God is sin—so also is abuse of the created order.

Within the theory of evolution it is possible, though difficult, to explain human sin as some kind of inheritance from lower animal ancestry. Man, it is claimed, will get better as he evolves. This explanation, however, is difficult to defend in the light of the information available to us daily in the media. It seems that man is capable of a cruelty to his fellow man which is unparalleled among 'lower' animals.

This interpretation of evolution would free man from the responsibility for his actions: they would be the natural consequences of his animal ancestry. In contrast, Christian teaching asserts that man is responsible for his actions as he is made in God's image. Mankind was made a perfectly free moral and spiritual agent, with the potential to live in perfect harmony with God and the creation. But we abused this freedom by exerting our own will over against the will of God and so we 'fell' from the perfection we once had. This rebellion against God marked the appearance of sin in the world. The fellowship and communion which we had with God was lost and thus we died a spiritual death. Christians believe that Jesus Christ was the one human being without sin, who lived in perfect harmony with the creation and the Creator.

11 IS GOD INVOLVED?

GOD AND SUFFERING

Misery and suffering are realities in our world. They affect rich and poor, black and white. A rich man can suffer from cancer or bereavement as much as a poor man. A black man can be just as horribly maimed or disfigured by disease as a white man.

A basic point has to be established. The fact that suffering is universal does not present an impossible problem for the atheist. He can explain easily enough why people suffer. Suffering is a problem for the Christian because he claims to serve a God who is the Creator and who is loving, good and caring. How can a God like that allow suffering, especially where the innocent are involved?

At this stage it must be said that there is no complete, water-tight Christian answer to this problem. All that we have is the outline of a possible answer.

Evil and suffering

Christians distinguish two types of evil—moral evil and 'natural' evil.

Moral evil is found in wrong relations with *God* and with what *God has made*, especially people. The two aspects are intimately related— in much the same way as the two positive commands to love God and to love our neighbour. Most human suffering comes from what is often called 'man's inhumanity to man'—the evil of not caring for others as we care for ourselves. Of this the modern media provide so many examples—war, refugee camps, selfish use of resources—the list is endless. In the end we may appear not to take them very seriously.

'Natural' evil is found in the effects on people and animals of distortion in the natural environ-ment—disease, earthquakes, tornadoes, flooding, drought and so on. Again the media keep us supplied with examples of this kind of thing, with heart-rending pictures of the suffering caused.

God and evil

As they read from the Bible, Christians make three basic claims, which must be held together in tension.

● God is wholly good and loving
● God is all-powerful
● Evil really exists in the world and causes great suffering.

If any one of these three claims is not true, then the 'problem' disappears. If God is good but not all-powerful, then though he may want to remove suffering he may not be able to do so. If God is all-powerful but not good, then though he may have the power to remove suffering he may not wish to do so. And, if evil is an illusion—as Christian Science and Hinduism teach—then what are we worrying about?

The problem of moral evil

The most urgent task for the Christian is to answer the problems raised by moral evil—if only because more of the world's suffering stems from this than from evil in the natural world.

The traditional Christian answer is called the 'free will defence', and it is the only one that holds up. It argues that the almighty Creator made human beings in such a way that they are free to choose good or evil. This freedom is an essential part of their humanity. God's plan was that they would use this freedom to do what he wanted and to offer him praise and thanksgiving.

The history of the human race shows that this has not happened

Handicap, disease, bereavement, natural disaster – they are no one's fault, least of all those who have to endure their effects. They cause great pain, however heroically it is borne. And they seem to fall at random, in accordance with no recognizable scheme of justice. Why does God allow suffering?

In the New Testament suffering is recognized as a fact of life, and we are taught how to cope with it. For example Peter wrote: 'Christ himself suffered for you and left you an example, so that you would follow in his steps. He committed no sin and no one ever heard a lie come from his lips. When he was insulted he did not answer back with an insult; when he suffered he did not threaten, but placed his hopes in God, the righteous Judge!'
1 Peter 2:21-23

Christians believe that God is present in this world of suffering. Paul wrote to the Romans (8:28): 'We know that in all things God works for good with those who love him, those whom he has called according to his purpose.'

This parable is told by Professor Basil Mitchell of Oxford. It illustrates the fact that Christians are committed to God and his goodness but they cannot wholly explain the problem of suffering:

'In time of war in an occupied country, a member of the resistance meets one night a stranger who deeply impresses him. They spend that night together in conversation. The Stranger tells the partisan that he himself is on the side of the resistance—indeed that he is in command of it, and urges the partisan to have faith in him no matter what happens. The partisan is utterly convinced at that meeting of the Stranger's sincerity and constancy and undertakes to trust him.

'They never meet in conditions of intimacy again. But sometimes the Stranger is seen helping members of the resistance, and the partisan is grateful and says to his friends, "He is on our side."

'Sometimes he is seen in the uniform of the police handing over patriots to the occupying power. On these occasions his friends murmur against him: but the partisan still says, "He is on our side." He still believes that, in spite of appearances, the Stranger did not deceive him. Sometimes he asks the Stranger for help and receives it. He is then thankful. Sometimes he asks and does not receive it. Then he says "The Stranger knows best". Sometimes his friends, in exasperation, say "Well, what *would* he have to do for you to admit that you were wrong and that he is not on our side?" But the partisan refuses to answer. He will not consent to put the Stranger to the test. And sometimes his friends complain, "Well, if *that's* what you mean by his being on our side, the sooner he goes over to the other side the better."

'The partisan of the parable does not allow anything to count decisively against the proposition "The Stranger is on our side". This is because he has committed himself to trust the Stranger. But he of course recognizes that the Stranger's ambiguous behaviour *does* count against what he believes about him. It is precisely this situation which constitutes the trial of his faith.'

though the results have often been, and possibly will be in the future, to remove it is to reduce humans to creatures living by instinct and not by choice.

Some people have also asked, 'Why did God create people with the freedom to follow evil inclinations? Could he not have made us in such a way that, however much we may desire and intend to do evil, we would be prevented from actually doing it?' But here again if this were so God would have made automatons, not people. If God made man to love him freely and spontaneously, then he could not make him so that he could only do good. For our love and worship of God to have value it must be freely chosen.

So while there are difficulties attached to it, the free will defence does begin to supply an answer to the problem of moral evil. Further, this defence can still be maintained even allowing for the tremendous pressures which push people to do wrong and cause harm—pressures from environment, heredity and the devil. No one would deny that these powerful pressures exist, but yet each human being does still make moral choices, even if by habit or example he is prone to choose what is wrong.

The problem of 'natural' evil

If a man is walking up a mountain and a rock falls and kills him, his family and friends are grieved but they do not feel vengeful. But if the rock was deliberately pushed on him by a business competitor then they would probably hate that person and want revenge. 'Natural' evil does not bother us as much as moral evil. We accept it much more as part of the way things are.

Some natural catastrophes can be avoided by human action. But the presence of disease and the difficulties it causes cannot so easily be dismissed. Though small-pox is virtually eradicated, cancer and many other diseases remain, and these will be responsible for widespread pain and death.

The fact that Jesus and his apostles declared war on disease

People have used their freedom to please God and they have used it to harm others. And the evil of which men are capable and the suffering this can cause are amply illustrated everywhere you look in the history of the twentieth century. And so we can quite reasonably say that moral evil is caused by *people* exercising their free will. It is quite contrary to what *God* wishes.

But this leaves the question: 'Why does God not intervene directly to stop the deeds of evil men?' For example, 'Why did he not stop the brutality perpetrated by Hitler in World War II?'

We do not know the full answer to such questions. Part of it is that being human and remaining human involves the possibility of choice—choosing good or evil. Terrible suggests to the Christian that disease is not part of the creation God made and intended. Disease must have come into the world as a result of moral evil. But how and when? In the story of humanity's fall, the garden of Eden story, Adam and Eve were told that their deliberate choice to disobey God would spoil much more than their own individual lives—the whole natural world would be affected. Fertility would be impaired, pain and death would take their toll: 'I will increase ... your pain in giving birth ... the ground will be under a curse ... you will have to work hard and sweat to make it produce anything, until you go back to the soil from which you were formed. You were made from soil, and you will become soil again.'

The choice to be independent of God resulted in death—separation from God. It upset the harmony of all creation. This is why the Christian's future hope involves a yearning for humanity, nature and God to be brought back into harmony. As Paul wrote: 'All of creation waits with eager longing for God to reveal his sons. For creation was condemned to lose its purpose ... Yet there was the hope that creation itself would one day be set free from its slavery to decay and would share the glorious freedom of the children of God.'

Of course just *how* moral evil is connected with this universal natural catastrophe will always remain a mystery. But seemingly the fruitfulness and cohesion of the created order were held in being by God in a way that relied on all of it being totally dependent on him.

Why does suffering appear so haphazard?

Both good and bad people suffer, for we are all part of the same human race living on the same earth. As the rain falls and the sun shines on both good and bad, so suffering comes upon all types of people. In the last analysis only God can answer the question why one man suffers when another does not.

But the situation is not without hope. It is because suffering falls so haphazardly that it provokes feelings of sympathy and compassion for its victims. If each time a person was struck down with an incurable disease or injured in an accident we could say it was a just punishment for his sins, then human suffering would soon be met with a shrug of the shoulders. But Jesus made it clear that this is *not* so. Suffering may be a result of the presence of sin and evil in the world. It is *not* a result of a person's own sin.

One of the intriguing aspects of suffering is that very often it is a worse experience for those looking on than for the one actually undergoing it. Sometimes there is a mysterious power at work in those who suffer which their friends find baffling. This serves to remind us that evil and suffering pose a problem because Christians believe in a good God who is active in creation and in the lives of his people. God himself did not remain aloof from suffering, but in the person of Jesus of Nazareth entered the world and endured pain of mind and body on our behalf. Even though the world has gone wrong, God has taken responsibility for it. Jesus died for that very sin and evil which has caused the pain and distortion of creation. He died the death due to us, and when we suffer he enters into close identity with us, as someone who has gone through it all himself. Above all, his death was 'for the sins of the whole world': he made it possible for there to be a new start, a whole new creation. His rising from death was the beginning of this—its fulfilment is still to come.

WHERE DOES THE BIBLE FIT IN?

Though the number of people attending church regularly is getting less in Western society, sales of the Bible increase. And there is an ever-increasing number of translations on sale—Living Bible, Jerusalem Bible, New English Bible, Good News Bible, New International Version, Revised Standard Version, the Common Bible—the list goes on.

People buy Bibles for a variety of reasons, only some of them religious. The Bible is an ancient book; it has many authors; it covers a wide range of literary form and style; it has had an important effect on Western civilization and it contains the stories of great men and women, notably Jesus of Nazareth.

What the Bible is about

Christians have a variety of reasons for reading the Bible, too, but one is basic and compelling. They believe it is the one and only place where we learn how God revealed himself to the world and how humanity responded to this divine revelation. More particularly it is the record of how God made himself known in Jesus Christ, and how this was prepared for in the history of the people of Israel.

The Christian Bible is composed of the Old Testament (the Jewish Bible, written originally in Hebrew) and the New Testament (written originally in popular Greek, the type spoken in the Roman Empire). So Jews and Christians have much in common.

The Bible presupposes the existence of God and describes his relationship to the world as its Creator, Sustainer, Ruler, Saviour and Judge. Always God is presented as taking the initiative in establishing personal relationships

with people. He called Abraham out of Mesopotamia, and led him to Canaan. He revealed himself to Abraham so that he could become the father of a people who would know God as their living Lord. Later he revealed himself to Moses, leader of the descendants of Abraham, on Mount Sinai and gave the details of a solemn agreement between the Israelites and himself.

And the human response to God's initiative is presented without frills. The good and bad side of humanity both come out clearly.

The way God responds to the prayers and cries of the people is clear evidence of his character. As they groaned under the hardships imposed by the Egyptian Pharaoh, the Israelites cried to God. His answer was a marvellous deliverance (the Exodus) which the Jews remember to this day.

These great themes of God's initiative, the human response and the concern of God for the needs of his people can be found in every part of the Old Testament. In the books of the prophets, for example, it is God who takes the initiative by giving his word to his messenger who then delivers it to the people. It is a word which includes judgement, comfort, hope and salvation.

Running through the Old Testament, as a golden thread, is the promise that God will send a great deliverer to his people. This hope was summed up in the word *Messiah*, a descendant of King

David, who would be God's unique messenger, prophet, teacher, leader, guide and saviour.

The books which make up the New Testament were written by disciples of Jesus who were convinced that he was this Messiah—and more than that, the eternal Son of God in a human life; God made man.

The New Testament is a proclamation of the good news about Jesus. The Gospels are not simply biographies. They tell us how God was working in Jesus to bring salvation to the world. The rest of the New Testament tells the story of how the good news of Jesus as Son of God and Saviour of the world was proclaimed in the Roman Empire. From those who believed this good news were formed the churches, groups of people who tried to live out together the Jesus life. As in the Old Testament, we find both the positive and negative sides of the human response to God's presence in Jesus. The New Testament church, for example, is not presented in idealistic terms but in honest, down-to-earth practicalities. The reader of Paul's first letter to the Corinthian church will see its sins and weaknesses as well as its triumphs and successes.

How the Bible was written

Since Christians believe that the Bible presents God's revelation to

To his assistant, Timothy, the apostle Paul wrote: 'Ever since you were a child you have known the Holy Scriptures, which are able to give you the wisdom that leads to salvation through faith in Christ Jesus. All Scripture is inspired by God and is useful for teaching the truth, rebuking error, correcting faults, and giving instruction for right living, so that the person who serves God may be fully qualified and equipped to do every kind of good deed.'
2 Timothy 3:15-16

● **Light.**
'Your word is a lamp to guide me and a light for my path.'
Psalm 119:105

● **Fire:**
'Is not my word like fire, says the Lord, and like a hammer which breaks the rock in pieces?'
Jeremiah 23:29

● **Sword:**
'For the word of God is living and active, sharper than any two-edged sword . . . discerning the thoughts and intentions of the heart.'
Hebrew 4:12

● **Milk:**
'Be like new-born babies, always thirsty for the pure spiritual milk, so that by drinking it you may grow up and be saved.'
1 Peter 2:2

● **Mirror:**
'For if any one is a hearer of the word, and not a doer, he is like a man who observes his natural face in a mirror; for he observes himself and goes away and at once forgets what he was like. But he who looks into the perfect law, the law of liberty, and perseveres, being no hearer that forgets but a doer that acts, he shall be blessed in his doing.'
James 2:23-25

the world, it is not surprising that they see God specially involved in its writing. They do not hold that each writer became merely a scribe of God. But they do believe the Holy Spirit was in the whole process of writing, so that what each man wrote was true to God's revelation. Each author had his own personality, style and vocabulary, yet God guided him to record the essential story of his revelation, and preserved him from making mistakes about its truth.

We can find in the Bible all we need to know about God so that we can worship, love, serve and obey him, and know we are doing these things in the way he wants.

The Bible and other holy books

Most religions have their holy books. Muslims regard the Qur'an with great reverence, and the basis of Hinduism is set forth in the ancient Vedas. Much that is in the Qur'an is similar to parts of the Old and New Testaments, but the ancient books of Hinduism belong to a very different religious tradition, which does not require belief in one personal, supreme God.

The basic reason why Christians regard the Bible as different from all other books is that they believe it contains the only true account of

the Creator and Saviour of
in this book is the
ersonal, pure
nd revealed
nly God is the
Qur'an and
ribe, but the
God needs
ring out its
nce. So
ily in the
New
d God
nd depth.
tians think
er religions.)

WHO AM I, AND WHY?

At times almost everyone asks probing questions about why they exist and what their life means. For many people these questions arise in a personal crisis, illness or depression. A few find their solutions so unsatisfactory that they give way to despair—even suicide. The majority soon stop looking for an answer and find some escape-route from the whole question—such as work or a fantasy world.

Each religion and ideology has its own answer. The Christian answer stands in strong contrast to other views vying for our attention in modern society.

Christians reject the idea that our existence is merely accidental

Who I am is greatly determined by factors outside my control. I did not choose to be born, in fact my parents may even not have intended me to be conceived. As a baby I showed traits inherited from my parents—brown eyes, big feet. Then as I grew up I acquired further characteristics from my environment—a particular language and culture. I cannot escape from the fact that I was born in a particular country at a particular time, went to particular schools and so on. The amount of choice which any one of us possesses is limited, and the poorer or less skilled we are the less is the choice.

Yet in the area of morality, each of us has choice, even though to choose what is right may be easier for some than for others. A girl can choose not to sleep with her boyfriend or not to have an abortion. Her friends may think she is foolish and they may exert great pressure on her, but still she can

choose to follow what she believes to be right. This moral sense is one factor in our experience which makes us ask questions about personal existence and the meaning of life. And it makes most of us dissatisfied with any answer which suggests we exist merely as an accident, or as a product of the laws of nature.

A Christian accepts that we are all made in the image of God, and can only know who we are in fellowship with God

The first thing that is said about human beings in the Bible is that God made us in his own 'image'. We are made to reflect some sort of mirror-image of the character of God. As the eternal Spirit, God is holy, righteous love. To reflect such a reality people must necessarily be more than merely physical, materialistic beings—they have a moral, spiritual nature. Man is a unity of body and soul, material and spiritual.

A person who lives as God wants him to live, enjoying fellowship with his Creator and doing his will, discovers his true identity. As he grows in fellowship with God he knows that he is a child of God, and loves to talk with his Father God in prayer.

A Christian accepts that we all need help to live as God wants and to enjoy fellowship with our Maker

The sad story of the human race is that we have failed to live in the way God planned. We have preferred to assert our own will against the will of God and to go our own way instead of God's way. Yet amazingly there is still much good to be found in all races and peoples. The basic reason why people care for one another and work to improve the world is that we are made in God's image. Though we are not living in communion with God, our moral nature still cries out for goodness, truth and faithfulness.

Certainly Christians believe that we are all sinners who do not love God and our fellow men as we should. We have lost the ability to have communion with God. If we want to know fellowship with our Maker, if we want to be the people he intended us to be, we need God's specific help. Christians are joyfully convinced that this help is available

> Augustine, the great North African theologian:
> 'You have made us for yourself, and our hearts are restless till they find their rest in you.'

as new life in Jesus Christ given by the Holy Spirit.

Through Jesus Christ comes forgiveness for sin and the way to find a real relationship with God the Father. By the Holy Spirit comes the inward spiritual power to enter this relationship and live in it daily and for ever. The very fact that we have minds which ask these ultimate questions makes us feel that there must be more to life than the haphazard effects of breeding and environment.

Christians believe that the origin and meaning of our lives can finally be explained only if we bring God into the answer.

A Christian rejects the idea that you can explain human life in purely materialistic terms

It cannot be a bad aim to work towards the creation of a better society—one with greater justice, peace and affluence for all. But if the pursuit of such a society means treating human beings as if they were merely superior animals, all of whose needs are basically material, and who can be sacrificed for the cause, then a Christian has to be against it.

Concern about people's material welfare is very important, but it needs to be accompanied by an at least equal concern for their spiritual welfare. In other words,

Christians reject the entirely materialistic teachings of Communism, because we affirm that a man has an essential spiritual dimension which can only be satisfied in communion with God. I believe that I am more than my physical body and brain. I do not know who I am until I find out what is this 'more'. In other words I only know who I am when I discover God.

A Christian rejects the idea that we are only a part of the great, unending cycle of birth and rebirth

This way of looking at life is basically Eastern, and Indian in particular. It is found not only in Hinduism but in the various forms of 'Eastern mysticism' practised in Western society. On this view I may be reborn as an insect, animal or reptile. At some point in the future I may break free from the cycle and achieve a state of permanent peace.

Christians teach that an individual has only the one life on earth, and it is a human life. In this life a man has the responsibility to use his time and talents for the glory of God and the good of others. After death he will meet his Maker to give an account of how he has fulfilled this responsibility.

Once Jesus Christ has brought him into terms of friendship with God the Father, a person begins to recognize who he is. He is a child of God whom God loves; he is in the family with Jesus Christ as his Saviour, Lord and Brother, and he knows that God is master of his life. So whether his work is exciting or dull, whether he is rich or poor, whether or not he has the support of family and friends, he knows who he is. He has an identity which gives his life meaning today, tomorrow and for ever.

12 A PERSONAL FAITH

THE VALUE OF JESUS TODAY

Jesus of Nazareth has always held a unique fascination. As a historical figure he has been more studied and written about than any other person. In recent times his life has been the subject of successful films and stage musicals. The date of his birth determines the calendar for most of the world. Festivals in his honour mark public holidays and celebrations.

His life is an inspiring example of love and humility and his teaching points the way to moral and spiritual perfection. His death as a martyr and without any threat of revenge marked a moving end to a career without parallel.

All this is great! His legacy to the world is immense. This man who ended his career on a Roman cross has much to offer today to people in search of teaching and example. Surely all fair-minded people will accept this.

But Christians believe that Jesus has far more to offer than simply teaching and example. In the New Testament we find the apostles declaring the good news that Jesus actually achieved something for humanity; that faith in what he has done can make people's lives quite different. People from very different cultural backgrounds heard this preaching—Jewish and Gentile, Greek and Roman—but from right across this spectrum came many who found the good news speaking directly to their needs.

From what the New Testament tells us, we can extract six basic, common elements of what the apostles taught. When we look at these six 'good news items' we find they are just as relevant to people's concerns today as they were then.

Promises have been fulfilled

Right through the Old Testament there are promises that one day God will send his appointed Messiah and rescue his people. The clear message of the New Testament is that now Jesus has come this promise has been fulfilled.

Today many see what goes on in the world as a meaningless jumble, with no consistent thread. Believing that God's promises were fulfilled in Jesus means that at the heart of it all there is something we can rely on. And if God kept his Old Testament promises, will he not keep the ones he made to those who believe in Jesus?

This happened through actual historical events

Jesus fulfilled these promises of rescue not just through his life but more especially when he died and rose again. The heart of the Christian gospel is what took place in actual history—at a particular time, in a particular place.

This means that Christian faith is not a matter of what particular *ideas* happen to appeal to a person. It is rooted in history. We have to make up our minds whether we believe certain *facts*, for which there is excellent evidence. Many people find this highly reassuring. It provides an alternative to going through life not knowing what to base our lives on. Faith that rests on Jesus' historical death and resurrection gives a secure foundation for our whole life and personality.

Jesus is the universal Lord

When God raised Jesus from death, he exalted him as Lord of everyone and everything. The resurrection showed that Jesus was not just a great man, but the living Son of God himself. As the apostle Paul wrote, 'For Christ died and rose to life again in order to be the Lord of the living and of the dead.'

One of the most disturbing aspects of the modern way of looking at things is that life is broken up into fragments. Science and technology; beauty and the arts; political and social concerns; loving relationships; how we live from day to day—all are in separate compartments in our thinking. They do not form a unified whole. *But*, if Jesus is supreme over the whole of life, then he holds every part of it together in one. Life makes sense and is all of a piece once a person comes to believe that Jesus Christ is Lord.

Jesus is with us by the Holy Spirit

No one is interested these days in spiritual ideas that are purely abstract. And so no approach to Christianity restricted entirely to its historical side begins to be adequate. We need a faith that makes a difference to our lives here and now, part of our real life experience.

Those early Christians were convinced that they had not lost Jesus after his ascension. He was no longer among them visibly, but spiritually they experienced his presence and power wherever they were. And those who saw and heard them were convinced that their message was true, not only by the force of what they said, but also by the evident change in their lives. When a person believes in Jesus, he comes into real relationship with him through his Holy Spirit.

PROMISES FULFILLED

'Then Jesus said to them, "How foolish you are, how slow you are to believe everything the prophets said! Was it not necessary for the Messiah to suffer these things and then to enter his glory?" And Jesus explained to them what was said about himself in all the Scriptures, beginning with the books of Moses and the writings of all the prophets.'
Luke 24:25-27

HISTORICAL EVENTS

' I passed on to you what I received, which is of the greatest importance: that Christ died for our sins, as written in the Scriptures; that he was buried, and that he was raised to life three days later, as written in the Scriptures.'
1 Corinthians 15:3-4

JESUS IS LORD

Christ is the visible likeness of the invisible God. He is the first-born Son, superior to all created things. For through him God created everything in heaven and on earth, the seen and the unseen things, including spiritual powers, lords, rulers, and authorities. God created the whole universe through him and for him. For it was by God's own decision that the Son has in himself the full nature of God'.
Colossians 1.15-19

HOLY SPIRIT

'You believed in Christ, and God put his stamp of ownership on you by giving you the Holy Spirit he had promised. The Spirit is the guarantee that we shall receive what God has promised his people, and this assures us that God will give complete freedom to those who are his. Let us praise his glory!'
Ephesians 1:13-14

JESUS' RETURN

'Jesus said, "There will be strange things happening to the sun, the moon, and the stars. On earth whole countries will be in despair, afraid of the roar of the sea and the raging tides. People will faint from fear as they wait for what is coming over the whole earth, for the powers in space will be driven from their courses. Then the Son of Man will appear, coming in a cloud with great power and glory. When these things begin to happen, stand up and raise your heads, because your salvation is near".'
Luke 21:25-28

FORGIVENESS

'Everyone has sinned and is far away from God's saving presence. But by the free gift of God's grace all are put right with him through Christ Jesus, who sets them free. God offered him, so that by his death he should become the means by which people's sins are forgiven through their faith in him.'
Romans 3:23-25

Jesus will return

This was a promise Jesus made frequently, and his followers repeated the promise. History will not just go on and on repeating itself; it had a beginning when God created all things, and it will have an end when Jesus returns as humanity's Lord and Judge.

This belief gives purpose to our existence. The loss of faith in God has condemned many people to a depressing sense of pointlessness in life. But, if Jesus is true to his promise, we are going somewhere and our lives mean something. There is a goal and a purpose at the end of a road anyone can join.

We can receive forgiveness and new life

The gospel which the apostles preached is not simply about a new way of living—through Jesus' death and resurrection a new relationship with God is offered to us. We no longer need to feel alienated and excluded from a real knowledge of God; Jesus died to re-open the way to relationship between people and God. Through him we can know forgiveness and that experience of God for which we were made.

This gospel, the good news of salvation by faith in the free gift of God through Jesus Christ, has met the deepest needs of people in every generation. The drawback in all other religions and philosophies is that, at the end of the day, we are left to find our salvation by our own efforts. How can this be the solution, when the problem is the sinfulness of our own human nature? But authentic Christianity puts us in touch with a source of love and life beyond ourselves and restores in us the humanity we always reach for but know we have lost.

12 A PERSONAL FAITH

DOES FAITH JUST HAPPEN?

'I wish I had your faith.' How often do Christians hear that said? Faith, by this reckoning, is rather like blond hair or broad shoulders—an asset bestowed at birth. But nothing could be more mistaken. Faith, as the Bible understands it, is available to anyone—free.

What is faith?

Faith is at the heart of Christianity. But it is also something we use often in everyday life. Why do we stand at a bus stop unless we believe (have faith) that a bus will stop there on its way to where we want to go? And when (finally) it comes, we show that this faith is real by stepping on and letting it take us there. So to have faith is to be willing to act on good evidence.

But of course this practical example only goes part way to illustrate Christian faith. Because faith in Jesus is belief in a *person*, the best parallels come from when we put our trust in someone we know to be trustworthy. When we enter into a deep relationship with another person, there are always risks involved. Whenever we open ourselves to other people enough to let them enrich us, we give them the power to hurt us too. Why do we do it then? Surely because we trust them, we believe that they are worth knowing at a deep level, and that they will use our trust to build and not to break us.

In precisely the same way, a Christian has faith in Jesus because he is *attracted to him* (thinks him worth knowing), and *believes his word* (finds him trustworthy). The attraction lies in all Jesus shows us about what God is like and how he means us to live. In his teaching and in his ministry, he always put love at the centre of life, and assured us that to put love for God and for our neighbours in the highest place is to find life at its richest.

If this is true, it is wonderful. But is it true? We will only be sure enough about that to stake our lives on it if we come to see Jesus as *trustworthy*. There are some key questions to ask ourselves about his trustworthiness. The man we read about in the Gospels claimed to love mankind. Is his death sufficient proof of that love? He promised he would rise again. Do we believe the evidence that he did?

Faith in Jesus, then, involves believing his promise that to know him is to find a better life. And it means taking this belief beyond the mere assent of our minds ('I believe this bus goes to town'), to the point of being ready to prove it in experience ('I'll step on it and go there').

How does faith begin?

You often meet people who nearly became Christians, but then came up against a barrier they have never managed to cross. It happens like this: a person is genuinely drawn to Jesus, wants it to be true that 'his words are life'. But then he starts asking himself whether he is *really sure* that he believes Jesus' teaching can be relied on. Is he sure enough about it to start living his life in a quite different way? There is no final answer to this question. And so there the poor person is stuck, and eventually he quietly abandons the question. What this person was looking for was not faith but certainty. While faith never flies in the face of reason, it does need to reach beyond it. There is no such thing as total proof of the truth about Jesus *from outside a relationship with him*. You are only in a position to be wholly convinced of someone's reliability once you have known him for a while. Before you start the relationship, you can only believe it is very probable he is trustworthy. Many, many people who have looked carefully at the Gospel accounts of Jesus' life and teaching believe it very probable that he really is who he claimed to be, and can really do for us what he promised. But how does this *belief*

'Jesus said
"Ask, and you will receive; seek, and you will find; knock, and the door will be opened to you. For everyone who asks will receive, and anyone who seeks will find, and the door will be opened to him who knocks."'
Matthew 7:7-8

The writer to the Hebrews summed up the crucial place faith holds: 'No one can please God without faith, for whoever comes to God must have faith that God exists and will reward those who seek him.'
Hebrews 11:6

about Jesus advance into *faith in* him?

The answer is, when a person starts to relate to Jesus as to a real person—because this is the way he is. Speak to him as to an invisible friend. Tell him that, if he is really able to forgive people, you want to be forgiven; that, if it is true he can make people's lives new and different, you would like him to do so for you. In other words, stop trying to screw yourself up to believe and ask Jesus simply to take over. We all know it is impossible to hold on to our own complete independence at the same time as committing ourselves to a deep relationship with another person. And it is equally impossible to 'find faith' in a detached way, without letting Jesus near enough to convince us of his trustworthiness.

'Let go and let God' was Martin Luther's great formula for faith. 'I found my heart strangely warmed,' said John Wesley. Faith is God's gift to us, and if we want it we have to be ready to receive it.

A life of faith

Jesus sometimes compared faith to a seed—a tiny thing, but it grows. This plainly makes sense. When a person first puts his trust in Jesus, of course his faith will be small. He has only just begun to get to know him. That small faith needs to grow—and will grow, if it is genuinely faith in Jesus. People are not always reliable, and trust within a relationship between ordinary,

fallible people will sometimes be stretched, occasionally broken. But we will find Jesus to be totally trustworthy. The longer we know him, the more deeply we will trust him.

The things that deepen our faith are the same as with any relationship that continues over the years. Each time we trust him and act on that trust, we prove his reliability and trust him more next time. Whenever we fail him (as inevitably we shall), and find he forgives us and still loves us, our gratitude to him will grow more whole-hearted. When it comes home to us that we can be ourselves with him—doubt, anger and all, without fear of rejection, we will realize how deep his love is. Until, imperceptibly, we discover that our original infant faith has developed into a mature trust—not yet full-grown, as we still have so much more of Jesus to learn, but sufficient to be able to say with the apostle Paul, 'I know in whom I have trusted, and I feel sure he is able to keep safe ... what he has entrusted to me.'

Sudden or gradual?

Some people get wed after a whirlwind romance, others marry their childhood sweetheart. And, while some people find faith in Jesus as a sudden flowering, perhaps at the time of some crisis or turning-point in their lives, others take longer about it. But one thing is common to everyone who has Christian faith: none of us think of faith as our own achievement. Faith is freely given us by God, and we experience it as a personal, life-changing relationship with Jesus.

IS A CHRISTIAN LIFE POSSIBLE?

There are a number of different problems which may bring people to ask this question. One person may have been reading Jesus' Sermon on the Mount. 'I can see how fine it would be to live that way,' he says, 'but it is a very demanding standard. Could I ever keep to it in actual everyday life?'

Another person may believe he is a Christian, and just be at the point of discovering how deep the challenge of Jesus goes. From time to time he falls to doubting whether he can possibly keep it up.

Or another, seeing an apparent conflict between Christian ideals and our affluent, technological society, may ask himself: 'How do you interpret this simple, direct teaching in the complex world of today?'

A Christian life *is* possible today—but a perfect Christian life is not. This reply needs filling out a little.

Jesus calls us to a perfect Christian life

Jesus actually said: 'You must be perfect—just as your Father in heaven is perfect.' Yet he also taught the disciples to pray, 'Forgive us the wrongs we have done.' In other words perfection stands before us as a goal. But Jesus knows we will not be perfect yet.

The apostles teach the same principle. Peter told his readers to 'be holy in all that you do, just as God who called you is holy'. Yet he knew they still had a long way to go on God's way: 'Do your best to add goodness to your faith; to your goodness add knowledge; to your knowledge add self-control.'

John wrote that 'whoever is a child of God does not continue to sin, for God's very nature is in him;

and because God is his Father, he cannot continue to sin'. Yet in the same letter: 'If we say we have no sin, we deceive ourselves, and there is no truth in us. But if we confess our sins to God, he will keep his promise and do what is right: he will forgive us our sins and purify us from all wrongdoing.'

If the aim of the Christian life were less than perfection, both the reality and the attractiveness of Christianity would disappear. Moral and spiritual perfection must always be our goal, because that is what we will reach in the life of the age to come.

We know that perfection is possible in this evil world—Jesus achieved it. But for most of us it is still far away. We begin our Christian lives with a self-centredness which has taken years to develop. This is not easily removed. And so the life of faith is a process of gradually overcoming an inner pull towards sin. We often fail, and this is why we need God's forgiveness so much.

Thus Christians live with the tension between aiming at perfection and knowing they do not achieve it. Yet strangely this does not lead to frustration. When our hearts are sincerely set on pleasing God then, despite setbacks and failures, we find a wonderful joy and peace.

The Christian life is only possible with the Holy Spirit's help

God expects nobody to live the Christian life in his own strength. Of course we must strive to live as Christians. But the Holy Spirit is given to help us in our striving to live for Christ in the world.

How does God's help come to the believer? It comes to us directly as the Holy Spirit gives strength to our hearts, minds and wills. It also comes in a more indirect way with the natural fellowship and worship of the Christian community. God helps the believer in so many ways. He strengthens us to pray, to praise, to worship, to love fellow Christians and to love our enemies, to stand up for Christ in the world

Jesus put things very directly:
'Go in through the narrow gate, because the gate to hell is wide and the road that leads to it is easy, and there are many who travel it. But the gate to life is narrow and the way that leads to it is hard, and there are few people who find it.'
Matthew 6:13-14

and to keep a joyful hope of the glorious life to come.

The apostle Paul sets a very high value on the help the Spirit gives us. He describes the Christian life as 'living in the Spirit' and 'walking in the Spirit'. He calls Christians to 'be filled with the Spirit'

The Christian life is normally lived within the fellowship of a Christian congregation

God does not want Christians to live in isolation. When Jesus called men and women to be his disciples, he drew them into a group. He encouraged them to serve God together, to strengthen each other and to lead his mission in the world. He founded his church, which he said must exist on earth until the end of the age. And the idea of the church is so crucially important for the New Testament writers that they use no less than ninety different word-pictures to describe it—images like 'the household of God', 'the body of Christ', 'a royal priesthood', 'a spiritual temple'.

The New Testament depicts the Christian life as being nourished and enriched within the fellowship and worship of the Christian family. It is not merely the pastor teaching us; we all have a ministry to each other. This can range from visiting the elderly to teaching children. Our faith is strengthened both by the service we give and by the help we receive. We have the direct experience of God in personal prayer and meditation, and we have the indirect (but still very real) experience of God within the fellowship and service of the Christian family.

Certainly there are many circumstances where a person has

to be a Christian alone. He is alone each day as he faces people and situations. But he has far more chance of facing them successfully if his faith is strengthened within the fellowship of Christians.

The Christian life is not always easy

To present the Christian life as easy or straightforward is totally unrealistic. In some places to be a Christian is to invite persecution; in others it is to court social dislocation.

If we take our faith seriously in every part of our lives, then we will find some difficult problems to work out. It is one thing to interpret Jesus' moral teaching at a person-to-person level, but much harder when you are dealing with economic, social and political questions in the complex, inter-related modern world. And so you find sincere Christians supporting different political parties, and occupying both sides of the fence on issues such as unilateral disarmament.

Being a Christian does not absolve a person from the trials of life or the consequences of other people's actions. This is why Jesus described discipleship as 'taking up the cross' to follow him. What God does promise is his blessing, help and guidance through the difficulties of life. We are not provided with ready-made answers to all questions and problems, and we are not allowed to resign from the human race with all its tensions. But God undertakes to help the believer to find peace in the storm, to find light in the darkness.